TENDERING

AND

CONTRACTING

GUIDELINES

BY
Ahkam AL Taee

TENDERING AND CONTRACTING GUIDELINES

iUniverse books may be ordered through booksellers or by contacting:

iUniverse
1663 Liberty Drive
Bloomington, IN 47403
www.iuniverse.com
844-349-9409

ISBN: 978-1-6632-3172-7 (sc)
ISBN: 978-1-6632-3173-4 (e)

Library of Congress Control Number: 2021923039

Print information available on the last page.

iUniverse rev. date: 11/10/2021

CONTENTS

ACKNOWLEDGMENTS

Let me take this opportunity to thank several .First, my mother and father for all their hard work as my first teacher. This project would never have been completed without you.

I must also mention my colleagues and any instructors who guided and supported me through. In addition, all those deserving of thanks and recognition.

Finally, as always (my wife, sons and daughter, who) are most deserving of acknowledgement for their patience, love, encouragement, and support.

PREFACE

This book provides a practical guide to various services agreements and transactions. It is not a legal textbook but a useful tool for procurement and contracts officers.

The book is designed to be ready desk reference for reviewing, understanding, negotiating or preparing a range of practical agreements and documents. The information and guidance contained herein are only matters to consider. It should not be treated as a comprehensive guide on all subjects. Some terms and conditions can be amended to reflect your particular circumstances and scope of services.

I hope you, the reader, will find this book practical is not a substitute for legal advice.

ABOUT THE AUTHOR

Ahkam Mohammed AL Taee, has B.Sc. degree in " Mechanical Engineering" from Mosul University,Iraq in 1971.He then got M.Sc. degree in Machine Tool Technology from Birmingham University, " UK" in 1975.

-Admitted as a Charter Engineer of Iraqi Union of Engineers in 1992.

-Admitted as a Professional Engineer of Board of Engineers Malaysia in1997

- Admitted as a Professional Engineer of PEO in Ontario-Canada in 2007.

He has extensive experience in both the private and public sectors in a cross section of industries ranging from oil and gas market to utility power and water in different disciplines like maintenance, construction and design.

He has also worked within a supply chain management for sixteen years in different countries. This includes gaining experience in preparing tenders, reviewing expressions for interest, evaluating commercial bids, negotiating terms and conditions of contracts/subcontracts. He is also knowledgeable in subcontracting strategy, clarifications, contractual conflict resolution, preparing change orders/ claims, correspondence with subcontractors/ clients/law enforcement agencies. Finally, he is very familiar with the awarding of contracts using systems like Maximo, and Oracle.

CHAPTER -1

TEXTURE OF TENDERS AND CONTRACTS

Part- 1 Introduction

1.1.1 Why we make Tenders and Contracts

Tendering and contracting subject are vital in business. Well-versed staff with technical knowledge and in management experience act as guides to process complete tenders and successful contracts. This is how you regulate the relationship between the buyers (Employers) and the sellers (Contractors) whether the contract concerns materials or services.

All businesses, aim to maximize profits, by buying quality materials and services at the best possible price. This can be achieved through a good tendering and contracting process.

A trustworthy contracting process improves business-to-business relationships. Companies can share opportunities, and take advantage of each other's strength.

A complete and clear contracts help to prevent future disputes; clearly written binding terms and conditions will give all parties peace mind.

Contracts can increase the operational efficiency of any organization or firm. A stipulated deadline motivates all parties to manage their activities accordingly.

Contracts secure payments. No one like to be stiffed for work that has already finished. A legal document like a contract establishes compensation for services rendered and provides recourse when terms are not met.

A contract creates a legal obligation for both parties to perform specific acts, and agreement on their rights and duties .It is problem-solving tool. Parties often have the same goals, but different methods for tracking specific issues. Well-written contract bridges the gap, giving each party enough of what they need.

A contract drafter should have formidable powers of concentration, physical stamina, mental acuity, tenacity, the ability to multitask, and a sense of humor. They need to enjoy working with people and involved parties.

Another function of the contract is to define upon whom the various risks responsibilities. All parties should be allocated some of the burden.

1.1.2 Contracts History ([1])

Plato, an Athenian philosopher during the Classical period of Greece, founder the Academy, the first institution of higher learning in the Western world. That Platonist philosophy influenced English contract law's history and Roman thought. In The Laws, Plato recognized the same basic devoted little attention to forms of agreement, but recognized the same basic categories for cancelling agreements as exist today.

The legal system of ancient Rome was called Roman Law, including the legal developments spanning over a thousand years of jurisprudence, from the Twelve Tables (c. 449 BC), to the Corpus Juris Civilis (AD 529) ordered by Eastern Roman Emperor Justinian I. It is also sometimes referred to as the Code of Justinian, although this name belongs more properly to the part titled Codex Justinian's. Roman law forms the basic framework for civil law, the most widely used legal system today, and the terms are sometimes used synonymously. The historical importance of Roman law is reflected by the continued use of Latin legal terminology in many legal systems influenced by it, including common law.

In the 19th Century, the principles of economics, developed alongside the Industrial Revolution. This lead to the development of contract law, with the increased rate of exchange resources, all parties involved needed assurances that obligations and promises would be honoured.

Lump-sum contract is the oldest form of contract. The first book with "contract" in its title was John Powell, Essay on the law of contract in 1790.

1.1.3 Concepts of a Contract:

These concepts are the foundation of every contract and when properly assembled it will, express the full business deal. [4]

- **Representations**

A representation is a statement of a past or present fact that induces a party to enter into the contract. This can be made before or during the time of drafting.

A party may claim misrepresentation when a falsehood is stated. A representation does not form part of a contract. A representation may be an **implied representation** or **material representation.**

- **Warranties**

This is a promise that one party will indemnify the other for any damages suffered because of the false statement. There are two types of warranties: **express** and **implied**. There are three major subtypes: the implied warranty of merchantability (only given by merchants), the implied warranty of fitness for a particular purpose, and the implied warranty of title.

- **Covenants**

This is a written promise between two or more parties where one pledges to do something (affirmative **covenant**) or refrains from doing something (**negative covenant**). Real property contracts cover covenants., for any

3

covenant the parties must be competent and legally able to enter into a contract.

- **Rights**

A right is the flipside of the covenant. A right entitles a party to the other's performance. The rights of any valid contract guaranteed the parties to do their part of obligations like providing a certain services or supplying materials and more.

- **Conditions**

A condition to a scope of work is a state of facts that must exist before a party is obliged to perform. Besides the rights that are expressly stated in the contract, there are also "implied contract rights". These rights exist based on contract policies and laws. Each party in a valid contract is expected to operate according to "good faith and fair dealing".

- **Discretionary Authority**

This grants the party the choice or permission to act. The holder is not required to exercise the authority granted. Commonly, discretionary authority is granted with a condition preceding it. For example, a state of facts like "the inspection of the work done is done successfully so the holder with pay the price" must exist before a party may exercise its discretionary authority

- **Declarations**

A declaration is a fact as to which both parties agree. Sometimes it is subjected to the satisfaction of a condition. The declaration has no associated rights or remedies; breaches do not necessary lead to a lawsuit. This depends on policy and law. The definitions in a contract are considered a declaration.

1.1.4 Parts of a Contract.

Regardless of the nature of the services or materials to be delivered, a contract is between two or more parties should have the following parts; [4]

- A. Preamble
- B. Recitals.

C. Words of agreement
D. Definitions
E. Action sections
F. Other substantive business provisions (representations and warranties, covenants, rights, conditions, discretionary authority & declarations).
G. Endgame provisions
H. General provisions
I. Signature lines.

A-Preamble:

This is an introduction to a contract that describes the purpose. The word comes from "pre" meaning "before" and "amble" meaning walk. A preamble can contain facts about the contract. A data packet has a preamble, which the system needs but which goes before the data that the user will use.

The following is sample of a preamble of a contract,

Preamble:

A. Whereas the First Party desires to contract with an entity with technical, practical expertise and competence in the field of the services of internal design; and
B. Whereas the Second Party has the expertise, competence in the field of the services of internal design and has expressed its willingness to contract with the First Party to provide such services :

THEREFORE, the parties have agreed on the followings:

B-Recitals:

Contract recitals precede the main text and are referred to as the "whereas" clauses. They provide the reader with a general idea about the purpose of the contract, the parties involved, and why they are signing it. Recitals can be considered part of the preamble to the contract.

Recitals are not compulsory, but are frequently included in commercial contracts to set out the background to the contract. Contractual obligations should not be included in the recitals, but are more appropriately placed in the legally binding operative provisions. The same principle applies to key definitions.

The following is a sample of a recital of a contract:

WHEREAS

1. Employer desires to have Contractor to provide qualified and experienced temporary personnel to carry out specialised services, as described in this Agreement, Schedules, Annex (…) and Annex (…);
2. Represents that it has the experience, capability and qualified personnel to perform such services:

NOW It is agreed that:

C-Words of Agreement:

Usually beginning of each major contract, especially in the construction deals, there is an agreement; moreover, the wording must be sufficient to make a binding deal between the parties, which summarizes the act of coming to a mutual decision, position or arrangement.

Please refer to Chapter 3 Attachment No 1 for sample of Form of Agreement.

D-Definitions:

Normally, these would be listed in the 1st.article of general conditions of a contract. Definitions must be used to make the interpretation of a contract easier. They make contract provisions concise; the definitions are considered as a declaration.

The article of the Definitions is usually headed with the following text:

> Unless otherwise indicated in the context hereof, the following wordings and phrases shall have the specific meanings and definitions corresponding thereto:

The list of definitions vary and depends on the nature of the services / materials supplied. In construction contracts, the following definitions usually noted:

- Site
- Completion certificate
- Final Acceptance Certificate
- Sub-Contractor
- Release letter
- Day/Week/ Month or year
- Contract price
- Services
- Professional acceptance certificate

In case of education services contract the following definitions can be seen:

- Intellectual property
- Charges
- Student
- KPI
- Data protection laws
- Teacher
- Confidential Information
- ECAE's representative
- Representatives

A contract of suppling chilled water for cooling may have the following definitions:

- Agreed capacity
- Charges
- Connection guidelines
- External Transfer Site
- Premises
- RT-Tonnage of refrigerator
- Term
- Supplier facilities
- Chilled water connection
- Consumer obligations
- Event of default
- Primary network
- Schedule of maintenance
- Specifications
- Supplier obligations
- Connection date
- Extend transfer site
- Landlord
- Secondary network
- Plant
- Emergency event

E-Action Sections

This section of a contract shows and emphasises how to perform the principal objective and the exchange of promises. The two primary components are:

- ❖ The provisions in which the parties agree to perform the main subject matter of the contract, and
- ❖ The consideration provisions, generally the when and how and amount to be paid.

It will specially identify the obligation or the scope of the work and the value to be exchanged between parties, in some contract the Action Sections have a certain heading like ;Key deliverables,Milestone,Project timeline,Obligations of the contractor, Performance of services, Sub-contacting,Independent consultant obligations, Obligations of the Client, Contract price …etc.

These sections with its articles are very important part of each contract as it shows, the parties:

i.   Agree to do the scope of work.
ii. Agree to pay the consideration (i.e contract price).
iii. Set forth the term of the contract.
iv. Set for the start and completion dates

This is very complicated and detailed, particularly in service level agreements (SLA), the following is an example of part of an action section "scope of work" for one of the maintenance services of IT network which depends on the volume & complexity of the network. Usually it is divided into TEIRS like Tier 1,2,3 and 4, in order to provide clear & quantifiable objective standards ;

Tier 1

A Field Service Engineer performs level support on-site. The types of activities associated with Tier 1 support include, but are not limited to the following:

- Receipt of Service Requests from Customer
- Procurement of materials and maintenance of Spares to provide installation, Maintenance, and Quality Protection Plan (QPPCN) activities if such are included in this Service Description
- Spares Installation and/or replacement of defective Hardware, such as:
  - Voice terminals and wiring
  - Power Units
  - System Hardware
  - Modems or other data network products
- Isolation and diagnosis of Errors to distinguish them from building wiring problems.
- Working with vendors to cooperatively test and isolate network or other system problems.

Tier 2

Is defined as those activities performed by a remote Tier 2 engineer in support of the installation or maintenance of Supported Products including but not limited to:

- Remote system diagnostic and alarm support.
- Supporting and interfacing with Tier 1 Personnel
- Escalating to Tier 3 when necessary.

Tier 3

When escalating to Tier 3 usually done by" Regional Avaya Center of Excellence (COE) and the International Trouble Assistance Center (ITAC)" provide the Tier 3 Level Support through agreed back-to-back service span agreement with expert system.

Tier 4

Sustaining Engineer is usually remote personnel with in-depth knowledge of supported products and the infrastructure. The primarily objective is

> to handle issues escalated by Tier 3 by isolating and potentially resolving product defects.
>
> Incorporated with {**Tabulated agreed Response Time and Resolution Time to control all the maintenance work**}.

F- Other Substantive Business Provisions (representations and warranties, covenants, rights, conditions, discretionary authority, and declarations).

F-1 Representations and Warranties;

Usually before writing, any contract there is a tender stage, where the bidders ask/clarify and check all items /information needed for the services required. A pre-bidding meeting often is conducted. For example, if the main service was excavation of long trench the bidders will ask;

- What is the length of the trench?
- What is the depth and width required?
- What is the soil type in the entire route of the trench?
- Are there any pipes /cables under the ground?
- Are there any roads or other obstacles?

Here's, an example of how the Client may answer*;

- The length of the trench is 1km.
- The width is 3 m and depth 2 m.
- The soil is muddy natural soil; sample of 10 trials were excavated and cleared of rocks.
- There are no underground cables /pipes and no crossings.

Consequently,one of the bidder (XYZ) was awarded and a contract must be written and signed between the client & XYZ, the answers above can be considered a statements given by the client and the only way to include it in the contract as requested by XYZ is to use representation & warranties. How would you do this and why?

Representation is a statement of fact & the above answers are few present facts and other past facts, all intended to induce reliance. The representation that "the route has no underground-buried pipe" is a present representation while the "10 trials excavations" is past representation by the client.

If XYZ wants to have a cause of action for misrepresentation, they must actually have relied on client's statement, and that reliance must have been justified, if XYZ discover there is buried pipe in the route and XYZ relayed on Client's representation that "there is no buried pipe" without justification, then XYZ would not have a cause of action with respect to misrepresentation. XYZ would have cause of action, however, for breach of a warranty of that same statement.

A warranty different from a representation

A warranty is a promise by the maker of a statement that the statement is true. This promise will result in the maker of the statement (i.e the client) paying damages to the statement's recipient (i.e XYZ) if the statement was false and caused damage. That means in order to have cause of action against a representation, the contract writer of above example must use the following write up:

The client represents and warrants to XYZ as follows: *then list all the above statements (answers*) of the client.*

By this and as there is warranty (i.e promise) then XYZ can sue the client due to breach of warranty and the client is eligible to pay damage if XYZ finds buried pipes in the route.

As foreseen, any party in a contract can give representations to present and past facts, a party of a contract cannot give a representation with respect to future facts; this is called a **Statement of Opinion.**

To check any party's "Representations and Warranties", it is necessary to go through the following and clarify.

1. **Duly Incorporated**, validly existing and good standing:

Examples;

- XYZ, Inc. is a corporation duly incorporated, validly existing and in good standing under the laws of Commonwealth of Pennsylvania in United States of America.
- ABC LLC is a limited liability company duly established, validly existing and in good standing in Dubai pursuant to UAE Federal law No.8 of 1984 Concerning Commercial Companies, as amended.

2. **Due Incorporation**
   - If a corporation, LLC or other entity having legal standing is not duly incorporated, validly existing and good standing, then the party contracting with it might not be able to enforce obligations.
   - How do you verify this?
   - IN the US, and Canada, by Certificate of incorporation and Good Standing Certificate.
   - In UAE, by trade license, Chamber of Commerce membership and Commercial Register Certificate.

3. **Corporate Authority and Consent**.

Example;

   - XYZ, Inc. represents and warrants that it has all requisite power and authority to enter into this agreement and perform its obligations hereunder.

4. **Governmental Consent**

Example;

- ABC represents and warrants that it has obtained all governmental licenses, permits, consents and approvals required for the performance of its obligations under this agreement.

5. **Share Ownership, Intellectual Property and Other Assets;**

Examples:

   - The equity securities of XYZ consist of five hundred thousand (500,000) shares, nominal value fifty Dollars per share as of the date hereof, Sellers collectively are the record and beneficial owners and holders of all of the XYZ Shares,free and clear of all Encumbrances.

- Licensor represents and warrants that it is the owner of all right, title and interest in and to the Trademarks and the goodwill associated with and symbolized by the Trademarks.

6. Financial Statements
Example;

- The financial statements that seller have delivered to buyer fairly represent the financial condition and the results of operations, changes in stockholders equity,and cash flow of XYZ as of the respective dates of and for the periods referred to, all in accordance with International Financial Reporting Stds.(IFRS). The financial statements referred to in this section reflect the consistent application of such accounting principles throughout the periods involved.

In addition to the above examples there are other representations & warrants as "Anything where one party needs the other party to confirm the existence (or non-existence) of a particular set of circumstances".

F-2 Covenants;

With reference to the previous example of trench excavation in above context.

Imagine the contractor XYZ and the client have agreed on the price and XYZ tells the client they cannot start as they need a work permit and then site handing over. A delayed start the excavation is acceptable by the client and they agree to shift the start date of the work. This delay creates a gab period between the signing agreement and the start of the work

The contractor XYZ tells the client that they are concerned that the delay will allow for a change in the market prices of materials, the contractor XYZ wants to protect themselves from any changes or damages imposed on them, to overcome these concerns the agreement will often contain **covenants** sometimes called **promises**.

Covenant creates an ongoing obligation to perform, so the agreement between the client and XYZ had following covenants:

Client's Covenants XYZ
• Shall hand over the site immediately after work permit secured. • No delay penalties incurred for the time of delay due to work permit issuance.

Covenants often appear with representations and warranties, but sometimes they are separate from representations & warranties as in the provisions like: confidentiality, non-compete, non- solicitation.

F-3 Rights;

When there is a duty to be performed, there are rights for that performance; i.e if a person gives a covenant to a party then that individual will have rights against that duty in the covenant given.

The right is a synonym of the other party's duty performance as shown in below, (the car owner and the mechanic agreed to repair the car for a total $ 1200 with guarantee of 6 months of normal working condition):

Payment of repair price :The car owner shall pay the mechanic $ 1200 after completion of the repair.(shows here as car owner's duty) **Entitlement to repair price**: The mechanic is entitled to be paid $1200 after completion of the repair (shows as the Mechanic 's right) In both examples, the car owner must pay $1200 to the mechanic, but the difference is the focus: the car owner's duty to pay versus the mechanic's right to payment.

The duty and right do not always appear, like in this example:

> **Entitlement of Guarantee**: if the car owner drives the car without coolant & the engine jams, the mechanic will not offer the guarantee.
>
> In this the related duty is the car owner's obligation not to ask for the guarantee.

F-4 Conditions;

In order to explain and show the elaboration on the conditions in the contract, let us take the following example;

A successful deal between a contractor (XYZ) and a client, stipulates XYZ has to lay HV cables underground of total length 3KM providing XYZ have a certified cable jointers.

XYZ tells the client that they need two months to find, test and secure cable jointers for the deal; XYZ also tells the client that while they are confident in finding these technicians, and in this deal, the client cannot oblige XYZ to lay the cable if there are no certified cable jointers.

The client promised XYZ that if the cable jointers secured earlier then the site could then be handed sooner.

In order to reflect and secure certified cable jointer as a contractual prerequisite to XYZ's obligation to lay the client's cables, the service contract will use a **condition.**

A **condition** is an act or event that affects a party's **contractual** duty. It is a qualification placed on an obligation.

If that act or event does not exist, the obligation to perform no longer exist.

In the above example, the condition to the obligation and the obligation to perform might look something like this:

If XYZ obtains certified cable jointers, XYZ shall lay the HV cables.

The condition may be found in same section or different sections of the contract. There must always be obligations, if there are conditions.

Technically, there are three types of conditions, the first is the **precedent** condition, where an event that must exist as a fact before the promiser incurs any liability pursuant to it, as in above example this means the availability of certified cable jointers is.

The second type is a **concurrent** condition, where something must occur simultaneously with another condition, (i.e each party's obligation act as a condition precedent to the other), an example if cable jointers are secured earlier, and the site handing over will be quicker.

The third type is **subsequent** condition, where there is an action either (i) occur, or (ii) not occur so as to end something else., like" when the city closes its border, no visitors can enter".

It is clear from above example that parties use conditions to allocate risk, if we assume that XYZ did not find certified cable jointers, the condition is not satisfied and the performing party has no duty to perform. In this case, the client takes the risk that the condition might not be satisfied.

F-5 Discretionary authority;

The owner of discretionary authority has permission to choose courses actions within the law. This individual may exercise that authority, or not.

The following four examples explain how the discretionary authority is used. Like other contract's concepts, it allocates risk as well;

First; The warranty of new car.

Warranty. The warranty of the car is ended either at 100,000km or after three years from purchase date, whichever comes first.

Second: In house staff training.

Termination. Either party may terminate the training agreement by written notice if the number of trainees becomes less than 20 in any course.

Third: Lease of vehicle

Inspection. The Leaser has the right to inspect the vehicle, without prior notice, at all reasonable times during the term of this lease.

Fourth; Work Insurance

Insurance. A party sending notice to their consultant to provide either Professional Indemnity Insurance Policy(PIIP) or Commercial General Liability (CGL)

In first example, both parties the seller agent & the buyer of the car have no authority to act toward the warranty while the provision states clearly after the car reach the limits stated.

In the second example, both parties have absolute discretion to terminate the training contract if the agreed parameters occurred.

In the third example, only the leaser has absolute discretion to inspect the car but with less risk to the Lessor by stating "reasonable times".

In the fourth example, the parties have curtailed the exercise of discretion, the notifying party has discretion but with limited parameters.

Depending on the drafting of provision in a contract, the party holding a discretion can be either the party barred from acting or the other party. Check the following drafting:

Provision 1
Consultant shall not sub-contract any part of the agreement without the prior written consent of the client.

Provision 2
If during the performance of project, consultant finds a variation in the services, the client shall be notified in writing within 15 days of such development. The consultant shall await the client's reasonable instructions.

Provision 3
Consultant shall not suspend the work without the prior written consent of the client except under high-risk dangerous circumstances, during which the consultant must suspend the work immediately.

In provision 1, the consultant prohibited to sub-contract any part of the agreement, while in provision 2, the consultant has authority to inform the client within a certain period and allocate less risk to the consultant, as the client is to act reasonably.

In provision 3, the consultant reduces the risk to the client due to having full authority without constraint to suspend the work during high-risk circumstances.

F-6 Declarations;

A declaration is a statement of fact to which the parties agree. It has significance within the contract. No rights or remedies are associated with declaration and consequently a party cannot sue on a declaration.

All definitions in contracts are declarations they have no substantive effect, like the following in leasing in a lease agreement;

> **"The rental"** means $2000 per month.

An example of a declaration, which have substantive effect, is the provision of the governing law by which the parties must adhere to as per their policies. When the law is not kicked into action, it will be a definition (declaration without substantive effect) without right or remedies associated. [2]

> **"Governing Law"** the provincial law of…… that governs all matters with respect to this contract.

The declarations are subject to a conditions. Here is an example provision:

> **"Consequences in training"** The apprenticeship enrollment contract shall be in writing; otherwise, it shall be void.

G- Endgame provisions

They are for the consequences of a failed representation, condition, covenant, or the subject matter of the agreement. They will contain the remedies by the parties or liquidated damages. They are found next to the last substantive provisions.

Contracts can end either happily or unhappily. In either event, the contract must deal with the consequences of the close out. Some of the consequences may survive after the termination of the contract like confidentiality covenant.

The Endgame provision is written either as a condition to an obligation to complete a duty or the statement of the obligation/condition to discretionary authority or the statement of the discretionary authority, as shown below;

> **First**
>
> **Release of Performance Bank Guarantee**. After the contractor completes the work and receives final-completion certificate, the client will release the performance bank guarantee. *(Condition to an obligation & the statement of the obligation)*.
>
> **Second**
>
> **Submitting of Clearance Certificate**. If the employee does not submit his /her clearance certificate, the employer may stop the end of service payment.*(Condition to discretionary authority & the statement of the discretionary authority)*.

H- General provisions

These are the final provisions in the contract before the signature article, General provisions tell the parties how to govern the relationship and manage the contract.

Some of these are in the form of covenant. Other are in the form of declaration.

> **License Provision**: The contractor shall obtain all licences necessary to enable the contractor to do business in the country or countries and any political subdivisions thereof wherein any part of the services shall be performed.*(this is a covenant form)*.

In Procurement agreements, the general provisions concentrate on products, quality, price per unit, total value and currency, delivery, tax and packing .whereas in major construction agreements it concentrates on site management, material handling and project management. Often there are special provisions e.g. Restricted area and Hazardous area. We will see more of these in Chapter 3, Attachment 7 "Complete Construction Contract".

General provisions will have many articles like; duration, financial entitlements, warranties, variations, sub-contracting, applicable law, waiver, copyright, suspension, force majeure..etc.

I- Signature lines

This is the last article in the contract, which reflects that the parties signing the document agree to the terms and their contractual duties and obligations. Both parties signing the agreement as both make promises. In some contracts one party is signing who gives promises like in guarantee contracts.

Below the sample of signature lines write up:

In witness whereof, the parties hereto have entered into this agreement as of the day & year written above	
Signed and delivered for and on behalf of: **Name of Party 1** Signature; Title : Date :	Signed and delivered for and on behalf of: **Name of Party 2** Signature : Title : Date :

1.1.5 The Elements of Enforceable Contract (Valid or Legal Binding contract); [18]

- Capacity. Each party's ability to understand the terms of the contract.
- Offer. Have all essential elements.
- Acceptance.
- Competent parties.
- Lawful subject matter.
- Mutuality of obligation.
- Consideration.
- Agreement.

A valid contract should be mutual agreement on an offer and an acceptance, indicating a meeting of the minds. The offer must have a consideration something of value exchanged or promised by each party. The Latin word of "consideration" is (quid pro quo). Without clearly stated "consideration" on both parties, a contract does not exist, and neither party is bound to perform.

Both parties must have the contractual capacity and competency. They must be the age of majority and possess characteristics that qualify them as competent.

In addition, the valid contract must have legality, i.e the contract's purpose must be to accomplish some goal that is legal and not against public policy.

Finally, the consent of the parties must be voluntary. A contract cannot be entered into under "duress or fraudulently".

Part- 2 Types of Contracts

1.2.1 Introduction

There are many types of contracts; some reflect the work to be perform like; (construction, consultancy, workforce supply, financial and auditing services, and more).

Some contracts are based on risk, whether assessing or sharing them. Another type is based on the financial and payment entitlement method.

The following are the most common contract types; [6][7]

1. Fixed-Price Contracts
2. Unit-Price Contracts
3. Cost-Reimbursement Contracts
   - Cost-Plus-Fixed-fee contracts
   - Cost Plus-Incentive-Fee Contracts
   - Cost-Plus Percentage of Cost Contracts
4. Indefinite-Quantity Contracts
5. Time- Related Contracts.
   - Time-and-Materials Contracts
   - Labor-Hour Contracts
6. Letter of Intent.
7. Concession Contracts.

Let us go into more detail,

1.2.2 Fixed-Price Contracts

Description. A fixed-price contract establishes a price that is not subject to adjustment based on the cost of performance. The contractor has full responsibility for all costs and the resulting profit or loss. It is the least burdensome type to administer if requirements are stable; but may be difficult if there are frequent changes.

A fix-price contract is preferable because the burdens are on the contractor, which reduces the client's oversight workload.

Application. A fixed price contract should be used if:

- Scope, quality and timing of work can be easily and clearly defined.
- Fair and reasonable prices can be established at the outset.
- If the client supplies the material of the contract and can make them available in a timely manner.
- The level of risk for the contractor is manageable and reasonable.
- No major changes in the contract are expected.

If there is no reasonable market basis for firm pricing, the fixed-price contract may reduce competition and lead to higher cost because of contingencies added to protect contractors from perceived risks.

Whenever the probable cost of performance cannot be realistically estimated, a fixed-price contract should not be used.

1.2.3 Unit-Price Contracts

Description. A unit-price contract is based on the unit rates of a specified work component or time unites. Payment is made for the actual number of units completed. An estimate of number serves only as an approximate scope of work and assists in determining the contract value.

Each unit-price contract should contain a schedule of unit prices, a brief description of work, the estimated quantity or the time units, a statement of what constitutes a unit, and the price per unit.

Application. Unit-price contracting is useful when a complete job can be defined clearly into units of work, but the final number of unit required is unknown. Those using hourly or daily rates may be advantageous when the scope of work is impossible to define. The use of time unit rates, however, provides no incentive for speed or efficiency. Unit price-contracts should not be used to avoid defining a specific scope of work.

Because they can be abused, unit-price or cost - reimbursement contract provisions should not be combined with a fixed-price unless very different scopes of work are involved. For example, labor under one type of contract and materials under another.

1.2.4 Cost-Reimbursement Contracts

Description. Cost-reimbursement contracts provide for payment of allowable incurred costs. They establish an estimate of total cost and, sometimes, a ceiling cost, meaning that the contractor takes the risk.

Cost-reimbursement contracts are suitable when uncertainties involved in contract performance do not permit costs and quantities to be estimated with sufficient accuracy. Contract documents must state clearly and explicitly which items of cost are allowable.

Application. A cost-reimbursement contract should be used only when;

- Uncertainty regarding the scope and specifications prohibit the use of any type of fixed-price contract.
- The contractor's accounting system is adequate for determining costs applicable.
- Appropriate monitoring by the client during performance will provide reasonable assurance that efficient methods and effective cost controls are used.

1.2.4.1 Cost-Plus Fixed-Fee Contract

Description. A cost-plus fixed-fee contract is a cost reimbursement contract that provides for payment of a negotiated fee on top of the cost incurred. The fixed fee does not vary with actual cost, but may be adjusted because of major, significant changes to the requirements. This type of contract gives the contractor a minimum incentive to control costs.

Application. A cost-plus fixed-fee contract is suitable when a cost reimbursement contract is necessary but the uncertainties and risks are too great for the contractor to negotiation for reasonable cost-plus-incentive arrangement.

1.2.4.2 Cost plus Incentive-Fee Contract

Description. A cost-plus-incentive-fee contract is a cost reimbursement contract that provides for an initial target fee to be adjusted by negotiated formula, based on the relationship of the total allowable costs to total target cost, or the expected performance to the actual performance. This contract type specifies a target cost, a target fee, minimum and maximum fees, and a fee adjustment formula. After the work is completed, the fee payable to the contractor is determined using the formula. This formula provides, within limits, for an increase in fee when total allowable costs are less than target cost and decreases in fee if actual costs exceed the target cost. This change is intended to provide an incentive for the contractor to manage the cost efficiently. When total allowable costs are greater than or less than the range of the fee of adjustment formula, the contractor is paid total allowable costs, plus the minimum or maximum fee.

Application. A cost-plus-incentive-fee contract is suitable when a target cost, and fee adjustment formula are likely to motivate the contractor. The fee adjustment formula should provide an incentive greater than the full range of reasonably foreseeable variations from target cost. If a high maximum fee is negotiated, the contract must provide for a low minimum fee, or even negative fee.

1.2.4.3 Cost-plus-Percentage-of-Cost Contract

Description. A cost-plus-percentage contract allows for payment of allowable costs plus, as a fee, a percentage rate on the total.

Application. Since there is no incentive for a contractor to control costs in this type of contracting, cost-plus-percentage contract has very limited usage.

1.2.5 Indefinite-Quantity Contract

Description. An indefinite-quantity contract provides for an undefined number of specific supplies or services, within stated minimum and maximum limits, to be delivered during the contract period. It is for use when precise requirements for supplies or services, above known minimum requirements, cannot be determined beforehand.

Ordering. The period for and the personnel authorized to place the orders must be identified in the contract. Ordinarily, orders should be placed via written communications; oral orders may be made if they are promptly confirmed in writing.

1.2.6 Time-Related Contract

1.2.6.1 Time and Materials

Description. A time-and-materials contract provides for the purchase of supplies or services based on;

- Direct labor hours at specified, fixed rates (which include wages, overtime, general and administrative expenses, and profit).
- Materials at cost, and when appropriate, material handling costs. Material handling costs may include all indirect costs, including general and administrative expenses, allocated to direct materials in accordance with the contractor's usual accounting practices. This may include only costs clearly excluded from the labor-hour rate.

Application. A time-and-materials contract is appropriate only when it is not possible to estimate the extent or duration of the work or to anticipate costs with any reasonable degree of confidence. Because it does not encourage effective management control by the contractor, it should be used only when there is a provision for monitoring by client, to give reasonable assurance that there will be a minimal inefficiency.

Examples of situations in which this type of contract-might be appropriate:

- Repair, maintenance, and overhaul works.
- Emergencies.
- Engineering and design services in connection with the production of supplies.

1.2.6.2 Labor-Hour Contract

A labor-hour contract is a variant of the time-and-materials contract, except the contractor does not supply the materials.

1.2.7 Letter of Intent

Description. A letter of intent is a written document that authorizes the contractor to begin work immediately, before executing a formal contract. Its provisions are binding for both the client and the contractor.

Application. A letter of intent is to be used when;

- The requirement demands a commitment so that work can be commenced immediately.
- It is not possible to execute the formal contract in sufficient time.

Each letter of intent must be as complete and definitive as possible, state a maximum funding limit liability for the client and state a firm limited date on or before which will be replaced by formal contract.

1.2.8 Concession Contracts (Public Private Partnership or-PPP)

Government agencies are utilizing Public Private Partnership or Concession contracts, which are a form of project financing, wherein a private entity receives a concession to finance, design, construct, own, and operate a facility for a certain concession term. Many governments preferred to execute through the private sector to minimize their financial liability. Whereas some public agencies do not use them due to availability of proven alternatives and sufficient funds, or due to the existence of political barriers.

The emergence of public-private sector initiatives, such as Build-Operate-Transfer

(BOT), Build-Own-Operate-Transfer (BOOT), Design-Build-Finance-Operate (DBFO), Build-Own-Operate (BOO), and Toll-Operate-Transfer (TOT) for procuring infrastructure facilities and provides those PPP forms which are used for projects, that need high budgets, like construction of commercial complex using BOOT,powerhouses using DBFO; highways using TOT, dams using JVs, railways using BOT and more.

Below is summary of responsibility distribution of a procurement routes for PPP,

Procurement Rout	Traditional Public Procurement	BOT	BOOT	PRIVATE FINANCE INITIATIVE(PIF) • **DBFO** • **Joint Ventures (JVs)** • **Financially freestanding projects, Like :TOT**	BOO
Responsibility Authority	Public Responsibility	**PPP Responsibility,** risks and responsibilities shared between parties in accordance with their ability and strength.			Private Responsibility

PPP or- Concession Contracts have advantages like;

- Operational and project execution risks are transferred from the government to the private participant, which usually has more experience in cost containment.
- Faster project completion and fewer delays for infrastructure projects by including time-to-completion as a measure of performance and therefore of profit.

In addition, disadvantages, like;

- Risks for the private participant, who reasonably expects to be compensated for accepting those them. This can increase government costs.
- Expertise is heavily on the private side, putting the government at an inherent disadvantage. For example, it might be unable to assess accurately the proposed costs.

There is a well-known form of contract used in the construction of major projects called **design-build** contract, it is a form of project delivery. The client, under a single contract, with one entity (a **design-builder**) takes contractual responsibility for both the **design** services and the **construction.**

As **design-build** contract is relatively expensive, project managers usually use other types of project delivery. This is called **design–bid–build (design/bid/build D/B/B)**, design–**tender** ("**design/tender**"). This is when the client contracts with **two entities,** one for the **design** and other for **construction** of a project.

Clients, that wish to avoid retaining professionals, use the two above forms of project delivery. The works often proceeds either by fixed-price (lump sum) or by cost-plus-fee basis.

Part- 3 Acquisition (Supply) Chain

1.3.1 Introduction

To get qualified work performed with reduced risks, you need a well-drafted contract. This can be achieved through qualified tendering and an efficient acquisition chain, which we will discuss now.

1.3.2 Initiation of Tender Invitation Package (Request for Proposal-RFP);

The processes starts with a Request for Proposal (RFP) for which you need to have a qualified screened offerors (bidders) list. Later, their timely proposals are all evaluated technically and commercially with a chance for negotiations to clarify and complete the evaluation. This awarding of the contract to the highest scored bidder; through all those processes the **Scope of Work (SoW)** is the focal item;Fig1-1 emphasis the interlinking of scope of work in tendering process.

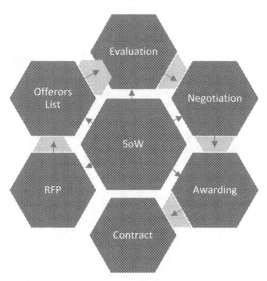

Fig.1-1 – Interlinking of SoW during tendering process.

The client or the requesting entity must carefully specify the followings: [6]

- Detailed Scope of Work (SoW).
- Proposed start date.
- Estimated contract value.
- Budget provision.
- Estimated duration sequence of work and milestones.
- Specific instructions and details related to tendering and evaluation.
- Type of contract/agreement required.
- Mode of delivery for the purchased materials.
- Payment terms,
- Other necessary information.

1.3.3 Scope of Work (SoW)

This is a statement outlining specific services the awarded contractor is going to perform, generally indicating the type, level, quantity of services, and the time schedule required.

The SoW is often weakest link to those involved in post-contract reviews. Not only is it a critical component (it expresses the desired output of the contract in legally enforceable terms), it often becomes the heart of (RFP), and the offeror's resulting proposal.

All following services need a detailed SoW:

Consultation services	Software development	Art & entertainment services	Aviation services & repair
Construction	Travel services	Design work	Trade show & exhibitions
Research & development	Fleet rental & maintenance services	Telecommunication services	Outsourcing
Environmental, health, and safety services	Land survey and right of way	Publication & advertisement	Inspection & test services

Janitorial services	Temporary help services	Ground keeping services	Lab services
Maintenance & plant services	Service Level or support services	Repairs	Capital equipment installation/ dismantling
Security guards	Facilities management	Benefits administration	Financial auditing
Catering services	Courier provision services	Credit card providers	Events management services

The client in need of materials or services must focus on the followings while planning and preparing the SoW: [6]

- Reviewing all requirements and documents authorizing the project. Including policy related to the procurement under consideration.
- Identifying individuals who should prepare or have input to the SoW–Cross functional team.
- Identifying all necessary cost drivers – The total cost of ownership.
- Breaking down the scope of work into parts, specifying service tasks, and describing the work tasks in terms of the performance data required.
- Preparing a list of items needed.
- Defining the order in which the work tasks should be covered.
- Identifying components of existing specification, standards, practices, or documentation.
- Noting the tasks, which require additional research or special preparation.
- Providing all necessary information and test results to reduce future variations.
- Obtaining assistance as required.
- Pre-bidding meeting with the invited offerors to clarify any ambiguities in the requirements of SoW before the closing date of the RFP.

Below is a sample of a performance type of "SoW "- for {Provision of Public Relations and Media services}, using the name of the client as "XYZ".

Scope of Work, (*for Provision of Public Relation and Media Services*)

The scope of work covers two strands: Ongoing media relations support and the development of a strategic communications plan.

1-Ongoing Media Relations Support;

Support XYZ's Communications Function to ensure rapid improvement initiatives are communicated to the key audiences. This is core to achieving XYZ's major communication objective or raising awareness of XYZ's credibility and role in delivering an (*...enter the business of XYZ, e.g public relation consultation*) system of excellence. Provision of media relations support, which will include:

- Two Contractor's staff functioning as a 24/7, 365 days a year, fully functioning press office
- Identifying communications opportunities and developing communication action plans to best position of XYZ.
- Development of press releases on key strategic initiatives
- Management of media requests
- Assess all media requests and provide recommendations on how to respond
- Preparation of key media messages around each announcement
- Development of communication materials for all media engagements (ex: FAQ, factsheets; speaking notes; letters to stakeholders)
- Attendance at regular meetings with key communications staff.
- Proactive pitching of stories to the media
- Development of deeper and wider media relationships on behalf of XYZ.
- Oversight of existing media relations function to ensure improved and widened access to all media
- Management of media at key events and providing media follow up following events

- Ad-hoc support for other communications activities as requested by XYZ's communication staff.
- Engaging with journalists to secure attendance at events and coverage in the media
- Managing relationships with other agencies that support XYZ's communication needs (ex: advertising firms; other official parts; external parties seeking XYZ involvement in events)
- Development of XYZ media management policies and procedures manual and guidelines
- Development of a communications crisis management plan
- Development of Corporate Welcome Kit
- Providing media training for XYZ's communications staff and senior staff within the organisation who will act as spokespeople for XYZ.
- Providing XYZ with access to Contractor offices in the global network (where appropriate) to capture media coverage internationally.

2-Develop and Implement a launch program for the XYZ Strategic Plan; Contractor will produce an action plan, which will include the following:

- Strategic recommendations on the approach
- Timing of announcement and events
- Messaging
- Outline content for each announcement
- Media Relations programme
- Stakeholder engagement programme
- Online programme
- Detailed action plan for the delivery of events and announcements
- Style and content of all visual materials
- Recommendations for branding and advertising
- Issues and Crisis management protocol
- Resourcing and Budgets
- Detailed roles and responsibilities for all parties
- Measurement

1.3.4 Preparing Offerors (Bidders) List

Developing and preparing an offerors list is very important because qualified firms will perform good work with no risk. If the client has no commercial register of qualified firms, they must evaluate new firms before floating any tender. The advantage of a commercial register is that it provides highly qualified and capable firms for specific materials or services required.

When the client has a commercial register, the following procedures should be followed; [5] [6]

1.3.4.1 Screening Process

When it is impractical to include in the offerors list all potential registered firms, a narrowing down of the field is necessary. This "screening" happens in two phases:

1.3.4.1.1 Preliminary Screening

All potential candidate firms from the commercial register are identified, with the type; cost and location of services are screened, but not all are invited to formally exchange information. The total group of candidate firms can be reduced to a workable size based on general knowledge without formally contacting them.

1.3.4.1.2 Formal Screening

When preliminary screening insufficient, and in order to ensure that only highly qualified firms are included on the final offerors list, the client should have the following current information:

- The status and interest of each firm, an outline of the nature, timing, and intended contracting basis for the job.
- The capacity (experience, organization, resources and financial status) of each firm.

Based on the above, the client can finalize the offerors list.

In a pitch, the offerors list can be waived when there is requisition for spare parts from original equipment manufacturer and overlapping works.

1.3.5 Preparing Tender Invitation Package or RFP

The objectives of the tender or RFP are:

- o Creating a level of common basis for comparison,
- o Gathering deep comparable information about firms.
- o creating sense of "urgency" in the mind of the firm,
- o Assisting with obtaining and processing large amount of information.
- o Ensuring that the firms selection process is objective and complies with legal requirements,
- o Clearly defining and communicating the specifications and the SoW.
- o Creating roadmap for negotiations.
- o Communicating the contract terms and conditions.

The formal solicitation of quotations (or bids) is done through RFP, the basis on which firms shall prepare their offers. The accuracy of communicating the exact nature of the materials or services required will significantly influence the quality of the offers. The client (end user) while defining the SoW must give careful attention and by supply management, they are prepare & float the RFP.

1.3.6 Contents of Tender Invitation Package or (Request for Proposal)

A complete Tender Invitation Package or RFP consists of the following documents:

1.3.6.1 Transmittal Letter; The Transmittal Letter provides a formal record of:

o Date of transmittal,
o Addresses,
o Sender Name,
o Contents of Tender Invitation Package or RFP,
o Submission Date and Closing Time for the offer,

The closing date and timing will also appear on the "Instruction to Tenderers" for emphasis.

It is recommended that the invited firms receiving the package should undertake a discretion or confidentiality agreement.

1.3.6.2 Acknowledgment Letter; The acknowledgment letter,if applicable,serves as a record that the firm has received the Tender Invitation Package or RFP and that the deadline for submission is clear and understood.

1.3.6.3 Instructions to Tenderer; This document is the foundation for the preparation of the tender, to ensure consistency, timeliness and complicity with special tendering requirements. The instructions, which are applicable to tendering for contracts and purchases, shall, where applicable include:

o A clear statement identifying the documents forming the Tender Invitation Package or RFP and defining them to be the basis for the tender.
o The object, scope of work (SoW) or description of services and purpose inviting offerors.
o The timing for preparation and submission of the tender.
o Specific instructions on the manner in which the commercial and technical bids to be submitted.

o   Alternative proposals that the supply management invites the offerors to submit.

o   Name of the purchasing specialist who can answer offeror's questions.

o   Arrangements for site visits, or pre-bidding meeting to be held with the offerors.

o   Weather, soil, terrain and other information, the offerors need during tender preparation.

o   Particular execution information and technical details.

o   The validity period which will formally be a suitable period after the tender closing date.

o   The tender closing date, timing, manner, and place for delivery.

o   The form of confidentiality undertaking to be signed by the successful firm.

o   Explicit statements stipulating that:

   i.   The supply management is not obliged to accept the lowest or any other tender.

   ii.   The supply management has the right to split the award among a numbers of offerors.

   iii.   The supply management will not pay for or reimburse any expense incurred by the offeror in preparing their offer.

   iv.   The offeror, if applicable should confirm their intention to bid-by-bid closing date and time in writing.

   v.   The offeror, if required, shall submit list of vendors and/or sub-contractors.

   vi.   Offerors are required to submit their tender strictly in accordance with the "Instructions to Tenderers".

o   The currency of the tender.

o   Whether the escalation formula will be permitted!, and the basis for any escalation clause.

o   Warranties, guarantees, and insurance required.

o   Statutory or official requirements for obtaining special licenses or permits related to the nature of the works.

- o A request to the offerors (bidders) to quote at several specific quantity or service /work levels with the corresponding value of each,
- o Any other information necessary in the tender.
- o Additional information for:

  i. Parking, marking, delivery, documentation and invoicing instruction.
  ii. Type of contractual arrangement, if other than standard purchase order.

1.3.6.4 Tender Security or (Bid Bond) and Performance Bank Guarantee Format.

Refer to Chapter 3 Attachments no.2 for sample Tender Security or Bid Bond Form and Attachment no.3 for sample Performance Bank Guarantee form, which is included in the Tender Invitation Package or RFP.

1.3.6.5 Form Letter of Tender (State of Compliance). A pre-printed form for the invited firms with details on the tender should include:

- o A great degree of uniformity among tenderers for easy comparison.
- o A clear statement by the bidder confirming that its offer has been submitted in accordance with the terms of the Tender Invitation Package (RFP) and indicating any alternative proposals or qualifications.
- o In major and complicated scopes of work, the commercial bid may be requested separate from the technical bid data.

Refer to Chapter 3, Attachment no. 4 for sample of Form Letter of Tender-or (State of Compliance).

1.3.6.6 Pro-Forma Agreement. For a contract, an agreement that supply management intends to enter into with successful firm shall always be included in the Tender Invitation Package or RFP. The Pro- Forma Agreement is prepared with blank spaces for amounts

or rates of compensation, delivery or other performance dates, and other relative details. Refer to Chapter 3, Attachmentno.1 for a sample Form of Agreement.

1.3.6.7 Evaluation Criteria. This is a very important part of every Tender Invitation Package or RFP. In major projects the technical bid is separated from the commercial bid,usually the technical evaluation is conducted by the end user while the financial (commercial) evaluation must be carried out for technically accepted bids by the supply management in coordination with the end user. Comparisons between all bids should be done to determine the ranking of the bids and the technical and financial weights. The final evaluation will determine which bid give the best total value of materials or services.

The evaluation report should have the followings;

- o Exclusion criteria, if any.
- o Evaluation criteria.
- o Maximum marks allocated against each criteria.
- o Score per criteria and total score for each firm.
- o An overall cut-off point below which firms do not qualify.
- o Reasons of disqualifying or rejecting firms.
- o A final recommendation.

Below sample of an evaluation criteria chart for the RFP of a provision of services scope of work,

FIRM NAME			A	B	C
	Firm Profile 15%	Score(1-10)			
		Weighted Score			
	PMO 15%	Score(1-10)			
		Weighted Score			

	Management 15%	Score(1-10)			
		Weighted Score			
	Technical 20%	Score(1-10)			
		Weighted Score			
	Cost 30%	Score(1-10)			
		Weighted Score			
	Presentation 5%	Score(1-10)			
		Weighted Score			
Total of weighted scores					
Comment					

See sub-article 1.3.7, for more detail on technical commercial evaluation and price analysis.

1.3.6.8 Technical Specifications. This document contains all the technical details of the work and / or materials including technical drawings and data sheets.

1.3.6.9 Delivery / Work Schedule. This document specifies the required time and mode of delivery of materials or services.

1.3.7 Selection of Best Total Value Offer

The main purpose of tendering is to choose and select the best total value offer. This is done with competitive bidding and making comparisons to the responses to the same solicitation, it is the best basis for price analysis because all offers were submitted to meet the same requirement during the same period.

In major projects, an integration of technical and commercial evaluations is necessary, there are cases where the technical offer is given high weight compared to the weight of the commercial and that depends on the sophisticated design and requirement of the project.

The project owner does the technical evaluation and has the responsibility to describe clearly what factors influence the technical evaluation and how that affects the price.

In routine cases, the technical and commercial evaluation will have 50/50 percentage weight. The commercial bid may have higher weight in some cases, like in routine maintenance services and standard supply materials.

Below is an example chart of technical evaluation criteria for consultancy services of major project;

Consultants Name	Firm 1	Firm 2	Firm 3
1 - Company History 30%			
Company history (number of years in the fields of Marketing, branding, communication…			
Worldwide Network importance			
International experience			
Number of years in Province…..			
Total			
2 - Experience 30%			
Experience in corporate branding			
Experience in building corporate marketing strategy			
Experience in Creative and Advertising fields			
Experience related to marketing Holding Company			
Experience related to Governmental authorities and defense			
Total			
3 - Team Presenting 20%			
No. of Members (Senior Level)			
No. of Members (Project Mngt. level)			
Presenters professionalism and experience			
Access to expertise			
Total			

4 - Presentation Content	10%			
Knowledge of branding methodology/ branding book/ implementation				
Understanding of Offset				
Ability to answer questions and quality of responses				
Creatives presented				
Total				
5-References	10%			
References worldwide				
References in ..*enter name of the country*				
References within the Public sector				
References within the industrial and Investment sector				
Total				
TOTAL	%	%	0%	
RANK				

Below is another sample chart of a technical and commercial evaluation with equal weighting for quality and price i.e 50 percentage for each with a cutoff or "Overall Quality Threshold" of 50 percentage. In this example, there are three offers (bids) from three firms for the installing electrical signs.

RFP no.			
RFP Title			
Quality and Price Scores for RFP's Bids Evaluation	Technical	Commercial	

Quality weighting	50%	Assessors		
Price weighting	50%			
Overall quality threshold	50%			

Quality Scores

Quality Criteria	Quality threshold - individual (A)	Criteria weight (%) (A)	Bidder(AA)		Bidder(BB)		Bidder(CC)	
			Score (0-10) (B)	Weighted score =(AxB)/10	Score (0-10) (C)	Weighted score =(CxA)/10	Score (0-10) (D)	Weighted score =(DxA)/10
SoW compliance		20	8	16	7	14	8	16
Presentation Quality		20	7	14	6	12	9	18
Design Idea		20	8	16	2	4	9	18
Material quality		20	8	16	7	14	8	16
Delivery & Installation		20	1	2	1	2	1	2
Total		100		64		46		70(*high)
Is overall quality threshold reached? (yes/no)				YES		No		YES
Quality Score (as % of highest score)				91.4				100

Price Scores

Tender Price ($)		256000		221505 (*Lowest)		618200	
Price Score = (lowest price/tender price)x100		86.5		n/a		35.8	

Overall Scores

Quality weighting x Quality score	50% x 91.4=45.7	n/a	50% x 100= 50
Price weighting x Price score	50% x 86.5 =43.3		50% x 35.8=17.9
Overall score	89	n/a	67.9
Value for money ranking	1	n/a	2
Recommendation			
Signatures			

The following is an example when purchasing a number of general items like spare parts, stationary, and toners and after receiving several offers. This either compares the prices of each item with the lowest price received of the same item or with the average price of the item:

Items	Offered Prices ($)			Stats			From Main			From Lowest		
							=(item price-M)/M*100			=(Item price-L)/L*100		
	Firm1 (P1)	Firm2 (P2)	Firm3 (P3)	Mean=M= (P1+P2+P3)/3	Lowest (L)	%Dev. P1=	%Dev. P2	%Dev. P3	%Dev. P1	%Dev. P2	%Dev. P3	
A1	2645	1577	2740	2320.6	1577	14	-32	18	67.7	0.0	73.7
A2	3830	3157	4435	3807.3	3157	0.604	-17	16.5	21.3	0.0	40.5
A3	11300	11369	14540	12403	11300	-8.9	-8.3	17.2	0.0	0.6	28.7
A4	3220	3020	1735	2658.3	1735	21.1	13.6	-34.7	85.6	74.1	0.0
This table is an example and doing it on Excel format is easier especially when the list of the items is very long, may have hundreds of items.						Taking the sign in the consideration, the lowest Dev% indicates the lowest item price among the other prices.			Any Dev % equal zero, indicates the lowest item price among the other prices.		

The above scenarios are often used to evaluate offers technically and commercially in order to choose the best total value offer. When purchasing general items you can split the requirement and award them to different bidders to achieve best value.

In sophisticated projects, the evaluation criteria's are split into micro items and each has a percentage weighting, giving the resulting recommendation more accuracy.

1.3.8 Negotiation during Tendering:

For any acquisition chain, it is essential and imperative that all the offers be confidentially and fair. However, there are instances where negotiations can be made, like the followings: [8]

- The lowest offer is substantially higher than the estimation, despite competitive bidding.
- The requirements of the waiver of competitive bidding have been met., like in procurement of spare parts or medications.
- There are special circumstances that make competitive bidding impractical, like in emergency cases.

- When the owner of the contract is seeking agreement on variation of existing terms and conditions under the contract.
- When negotiation is advantageous to the owner of the contract.

The supply management and concerned contract owner must form a negotiation team (or board), with team leader and authority to make concessions within the guidelines of good business judgment.

Pre- negotiation objectives and strategy serve as a general guide for the negotiation team during meetings with the concerned offeror.

In most negotiation, meetings the main objectives are good quality, attractive price, and quick delivery. These factors are interrelation; if you negotiate for affordable price, the quality may suffer, or the delivery may take longer, it is not always possible to have all three.

After completing the negotiation, the team must prepare a report that is accurate, detailed, clear, complete, and contains the following:

- Detailed results individually compared to the targets and estimates.
- Meeting minutes with the offeror.
- Reasons and justifications for any concessions made.
- Background of the concerned project
- Final recommendation.

1.3.9 Notes to complete the Tender or RFP:

As mentioned, any acquisition chain must have a correct, clear and detailed RFP document. Each RFP must have an exact title, number, name, and contact information of responsible supply management staff.

The following four documents are essential for preparing a fair and good quality RFP:

1. **Instructions and Information**, This document will have full information and instructions for the offerors which explains the purpose of the RFP and contains following articles:

a. **Introduction:** This explains works or materials needed with specifications, delivery and quality required. The instructions ensure that all proposals are given equal and fair consideration.

b. **Background;** The contract owner's background is necessary and this article will show their capacity to secure reliable proposals for the needed scope of work.

c. **Time Table,** An example of tabulated milestones is shown below:

Milestones	Due Date
Request for Proposals Sent Out to offerors	
Offerors acknowledge receipt and confirm their intention to participate.	
Pre-Bid Meeting	
Proposal Submission Due Date	
Proposal evaluation period	
Proposal presentation dates (*subject to invitation and only if required*)	TBA
Notification of awarding decision.	

d. **Language,** This highlight, the language implemented.

e. **Inducements,** This draw the attention to any type of inducement, which consequently disqualifies the related offeror.

f. **Ownership of RFP Document,** Usually the ownership belongs to the related client's supply management who floated the RFP.

g. **Proposal Expenses,** There is no entitlement to any expenses for prepared proposals.

h. **Confidentiality of Proposals,** This draws attention to the fact that RFP must be treated with confidentiality.

i. **Addenda and Revisions,** This highlights the procedure to process any addendum or revision to the RFP.

j.   **Permit and Licenses,** For any works or materials, the proposer must submit a copy of required permits or licenses, that secure qualified and accurate delivery.

k.   **Pricing and Currency of Proposals,** The currency for all payments is highlighted to reduce ambiguities, and ease processing.

l.   **Caution and Disclaimer,** This draws the attention of the offerors to check and verify the RFP, and /or consideration is given for error and /or omissions.

m.   **Firm Information and Format of Proposals,** The proposal needs to provide full address of the firm, the type of the firm, and any information that support the proposal,financial statement,previous similar experiences, summary of the organization chart and firm management, and finally the procedure to retain and submit the proposal with the,"offeror's response form, and required bid bond".

n.   **Bid Bond,** This financial bank guarantee is required for major projects and to secure qualified firms,(refer to Chapter3, Attchmentno.2 for a sample of Bid Bond).

o.   **Validity of Proposals,** Any proposal should have adequate validity to allow the client's team to study, verify and evaluate the proposals.

p.   **Right and Acceptance or Rejection of Proposals,** Detail instructions and conditions for acceptance or rejection of any proposal.

q.   **Non-Compliant Proposals,** If the proposal has certain part, item or condition not compliant with the RFP document,the firm should fill out a non-compliant statement like sample below,

Condition No	Details of Non-Compliance

r. **Indemnity and Insurance,** This details the cases and conditions for indemnity and type of insurance policies needed which cover any risks during performance.

s. **Signing of proposal,** This document prompts the offerors to: sign the letter of tender form or (state of compliance) in the RFP and the signature of the proposal and any resulting contract by fully authorize person.(refer to Chapter 3, Attachmentno.4 for a sample tender form or (statement of compliance).

2. **Statement of Work,** This document have following articles;

   a. **Scope of Work,** This is the main article in every RFP, it explains in detail the required scope of services or materials needed and any other information that makes the purpose of the RFP clear to the offerors.

   b. **Duration.** Every RFP sets up the required duration and target date to hand over the services or deliver the material.

   c. **Liquidated Damage,** Any delay in the delivery or performance without accepted reasons will cause the contractor to pay a stipulated liquidated damage.

   d. **Payment Term,** This is set clearly in every signed agreement as the processing of any due payment completion within the agreed payment term.

3. **Evaluation and Pricing Schedule,** This document explains the criteria for evaluation and the pricing schedule for contract value. It has usually the following articles;

   a. **Evaluation Criteria,** This article explains the compliance of the proposal with the requirement and specification, refer to sub-article 1.3.6.7"Technical Criteria".

   b. **Price Schedule,** This is designed accordingly to the type of the contract, below is an example format of the unit price schedule used in services or construction works.

SN	Description	Unite Price($)	Quantity	Amount($)
1	*Enter item 1*			
2	*Enter item 2*			
3				
Total Amount				

4. **Copy of the Contract and Form of Agreement,** Each RFP has to incorporate a copy of the contract/agreement that is implemented after awarding, and the requirements before signing. The bidders should confirm their compliance with the terms and conditions and identify any points of non-compliance.

Part- 4 Notes before Drafting a Contract or Agreement;

1.4.1 Introductory Briefing

As mentioned before, the parts of a contract need to be drafted to explain their purpose, and to state that the parties agree to the provisions. They should also clearly state the solution for any risks created and the rights and obligations of each party:

Name and Number of the Contract, Typically, the title of the contract should be written in capital letters to make it conspicuous through some are in bold and mixture of upper and lowercase letters. In public and private sectors, each contract has a number / year of issuance because the costs are from the fiscal budget and the expenses are subject to financial auditing.

Preamble, This is the introductory paragraph of the contract; identifying it by name /title, date, location, and the parties. The following is a well-drafted contemporary preamble,

---

This **Supply Contract**, dated as of March 10, 20xx . between ABC Education Authority located in……..(the "Client"), and HEWLETT-PACKARD EUROPE BV (the "Contractor"), located in Amsterdam, Meyrin Branch, Route du Nant d'Avril 150, 1217,MEYRIN 2/GENEVA, Switzerland ("HP"),

THEREFORE, the Parties have agreed on the followings:

Date, The following methods are often used in drafting a contract:

Version	Format	The Reason
1	,dated Febreuary,20xx	This format used when the parties reach agreement on the same day that they sign the agreement.

2	,dated **as of** March, 20xx	This format is used when the parties reach an agreement on the **as of** date, but do not sign their agreement until a later date.

This is very important because the effective date and signing dates may affect the accuracy of the representation and warranties or the covenants in the contract. Dates, it should not use to deceive any third party.

For example, On January 20th., 20xx. A builder (XYZ) agreed to build a house for client (ABC). On that day, ABC represented and warranted to process and receive the permit for construction within a week. If the contract is signed on February 1st., 20xx,without being effective as of January 20th.,20xx,then the representations and warranties speak as of February 1st.,20xx. In that case, the representation and warranty with respect to the construction permit is probably not approved. The construction permit may be not obtained or may take longer to be issued. Therefore, to keep the representation and warranty accurate, the parties should date the contract **as of** the date of their agreement. In this case of, January 20th.,20xx. Alternatively,the parties could date the contract February 1st.,20xx, and update the representations and warranties.

The same issue may happen if the **as of** date is used, because the covenant must be effective as of that date rather than the signing date. For example if in the above example the builder (XYZ) and the client (ABC) agreed on January 20th.,20xx, that the client(ABC) would give advance payment of no more than $ 5000,that covenant must limit the payment at that date. If the covenant (advance payment) is on February 1st. 20xx, the signing date, the client (ABC) may pay less without breaching the covenant.

In most contracts, in the signatures section there is a signature date that may different from the **as of** date. The drafter must highlight the execution /delivery/effective date of that contract to mitigate the ambiguity of the effective date. The effective date can be written in the preamble of the contract if it is not a future date; any future effective date must be written in action sections.

Parties, In any contract or agreement there is a consideration on which two or more parties agree on. Those names must be identified correctly, the right names can be found on organizational documents like a trade license or certificate of incorporation, After the names one should check the type of entity whether it is limited liability company (LLC) or limited partnership (LP) or corporation or cooperation or another type.

The names of the parties should be written completely, correctly with full addresses, telephone, fax numbers

Below summarize how and when the words (between or among) are used:

Between	Used for two or more partners, providing there is direct reciprocal relation with each party.	Example, contract between buyer of a house and the seller. Contract between a manufacturer and suppliers.
Among	Used for two or more partners, when there is **no** direct reciprocal relation with each party.	Example; The agreement of "Trade and Development Act" is among different import and export laws that have been enacted.

It is a general practice, that the names of the parties are written in the preamble, but now a days you can find contracts starting with the date, location and names of the parties that makes the preamble short and easy to emphasize the general objectives of the contract.

Recitals, if needed, these will follow the preamble, to emphasize the specific purpose of the contract and explains the relationship between the parties and why they have entered into a contract. This helps mitigate any ambiguities to third parties like courts or banks. Some contract drafters are using **Backgrounds** instead of recital. Below is a sample recital or background of a lease agreement:

> The Lessor has agreed to let and the Lessee agreed to rent the Premises (hereinafter "Offices"), which forms part of the *<enter the address of building/office location>*, *city name*, (the "Offices") subject to the terms and conditions hereinafter set forth.

With reference to the important parts of contract, the following notes, tabulated in sections for clarity and simplicity, covering the rest of contract details but not in sequence as in sub-article 1.1.1 "Contract Parts". These four sections help the drafter cover any risks initiated during the contract.

Section One, This section contains the **Form of Agreement**, (refer to Chapter 3, Attachment no.1 for a sample form of agreement)

Section Two, These are the Standard Terms and Conditions, this very important section has below articles that covers standard terms or modified conditions as per the nature of the services:

a. **Definitions,** a definition states the meaning of a word or phrase. Drafters use them primarily to clarify and prevent ambiguity, for example; they define "Business day" exactly while taking in the consideration the country location, as the business days differs. In addition, it used to explain technical phrase like "Completion Certificate" which indicates the contract is completed and closed out.
    In cases where the contract has many phases, the definitions article explains each clearly.

b. **Duration and Place of Delivery,** this states the start, and completion dates of material delivery or service performance, it is an article belonging to the action section.

c. **Goods/Service Quality and Confirmation,** this highlights the required quality of goods or services needed to meet the specifications and satisfy the codes and standards stipulated.

d. **Labelling and Packing,** this states the packing and labeling needed for any statutory or regulatory requirements.

e. **Intellectual Property and Risk,** All documents belonging to the services or materials delivered should be considered intellectual property, kept safe, and guarded from misuse.

f. **Inspection, Rejection and Guarantee,** this is very important article explains the required performance quality and the procedure to check the service or the materials for compliance or rejection.

g. **Waiver,** this is a party's agreement that it will perform as if the event had not occurred and that it will not exercise its remedies or walk-away rights. Waivers arise when there is a failure of a condition or a breach to covenant or warranty.

h. **Patents and Information,** this takes care of all documents,designs,instructions,plan, patterns, models and others involved in the contract must be retained and considered assets belonging to the contract's owner (client).

i. **Health and safety,** all services or materials of the contract must be performed and delivered without risking health and safety and being supported by certifications.

j. **Indemnity and Insurance,** to control and manage any risk or negligence during the contract term there should be this provision and it will be discussed more in Part no.5 "Allocating Liability and Risks".

k. **Confidentiality,** it is important during the contract term and after to protect the secret information.

l. **Variations,** any change in the requirements due to the work or materials must be calculated and approved by contract's owner and either paid or deducted from the contractor's entitlement. In some cases, this variation value is limited to a certain percentage of contract value.

m. **Recovery of Sum Due,** this is part of the financial entitlement between the contracting parties and is very important.

n. **Assignment,** this states who is entitled or not entitled to assign the contract, as well as how and when is to be done.

o. **Notice,** it is very important to state the method of sending notices, as well as the address and name of the correct contract person.

p. **Force Majeure,** This article shows the unexpected events if happened the contracting parties will be deemed not in a breach of the contract neither liable to other.

q. **Governing Law,** this very important article states the law to which the parties appeal if there is a dispute over rights or obligations.

r. **Suspension,** this gives the right to the contract's owner to suspend the work or supply of materials. It helps to stop unaccepted performance on the part of the contractor. Contractor also can suspend part of the work.

s. **Termination,** this gives the right of either or both parties to terminate the contract without breaching it.

t. **Subcontracting,** this regulates the sub-contracting by the main contractor under the approval of the contract's owner, keeping the contractor responsible for the quality of work performance.

u. In some contracts,you will see the following terms and condition like: (Security Compliance, Audit Access and Information, Third Party Rights,Warranty,Provision of "Performance Bank Guarantee, Advance Payment Bank Guarantee, and required Insurance Policies")

Section Three, the (**Scope of Work/Services**), contains all the details about the scope of work and the purpose of the contract with all documents and information needed.

Section Four, the (**Financial Entitlements**), are in the action section, which deal with contract value, invoicing, payment term, retention and advance payment (if any).

Part- 5 Allocating Liability and Risks

1.5.1 Introduction

The writing and signing of a contract is for controlling and reducing the risks, the written expression of the contract between two or more parties. Consequently, the parties need to agree and fulfill the terms and conditions of the contract. Below are some hassle points and guidelines to avoid them;

a. **One –Sided Protections**, If the contract is highly one-sided like a contract requiring the supplier to "obey all governmental laws and regulations affecting this agreement and the services provided hereunder", but not requiring the buying organization to do the same.

   The most reasonable approach to settle this issue to say," Both parties will obey all laws and regulations affecting this agreement".

b. **Ownership of Intellectual Property (IP) Rights**, Many buyers' contracts have articles, which transfer ownership of the supplier's IP Rights (patents, copyrights, trade secrets, etc). In some cases, these clauses are hidden within the document.

   Ownership of IP rights should be discussed between the parties before a contract is drafted, to ensure that languages reflects the agreement.

c. **Access to Source Code**, This potential "hassle point" is similar to IP right ownership but has some key differences. This issue specifically applies to software licensing transactions, which typically relate only to "object code".

   It is possible that if some licensees want to have a copy of source code by applying an "escrow" account just in case the supplier goes out of business. This ensures the licensees can continue to modify and use the software.

d. **Confidentiality**, Every contract owner should protect their confidential information, but it is reasonable for the contractor's proprietary information to be protected also (since the contract owner is exposed to the contractor's trade secrets too).

e. **Specialty,** Some articles are so one-sided that the contractor is held to a higher standard than the contract owner (buyer) maintains internally for their own employees who handle the same confidential information. A good example can be in the contracts of financial auditing services.

f. **Insurance Requirements,** Insurance is a contract, represented by a policy, in which an individual or entity receives financial protection or reimbursement against losses.

It is very reasonable for a contract owner (buyer) to require the contractor (supplier) to maintain reasonable insurance protections. For example, a commercial builder normally requires this from a consultant, and main contractor requires it from sub-contractors. In practice, the following types of insurance policy are requested; [3]
Commercial General Liability Insurance.
Worker's Compensation Insurance.
Employer's Liability Insurance.
Errors and Omissions Insurance.
Automobile Liability Insurance.

In insurance policies there is a very important issue which most of the contract owners requested from their contractors called the "waive of subrogation". Subrogation is "the insurer's right, after paying the claim, to pursue the party that caused the loss". Waiving of subrogation, means that the insurance company gives up this right.

This matter requires a lot of discussion and negotiations as if there is no waiver of subrogation; an insurer may pursue claims against contractors, sub-contractors, agents and employees. Moreover, whoever is responsible for the loss can substantially delay the project's completion. That may force the contractors to readjust their prices to mitigate the increased risk.

1.5.2 Types of Risks

In every contract representations and warranties, covenants, and conditions are all risk allocation mechanisms. Usually contract's owners have strategies in four levels; (avoid the risk, reduce the risk, transfer the risk, or accept the risk). There are many types of risks involved. Any contract may have tort liability, fraudulent inducement, or product and brand liability. The contract may have legal risk especially when there is a breach of conditions or obligations. The most common risks in contracts are the financial or credit risk, and the schedule or performance risk.

Owners should pay attention to any risk whether it is a strategic, compliance, operational, financial or market risk.

1.5.3 Evaluating and Categorizing the Risk

The contract owner must have guidelines for risk analysis. Then there should be an assessment of probability occurrence of the risk, after that the risk needs to be quantified, and identified. All threats and hazards should be placed in a matrix that categorizes the risks from high occurrence and high consequences to low occurrence and low consequences.

Then finally do risk/reward analysis: after collection of all information, compromisation is essential, as the client may not want to elevate the matter because the risk will might not occur or the financial consequences would be relatively small.

1.5.4 Roles that Mitigate Risk

Usually the following roles are using to mitigate the risk in contracts; [18]

- **The Role of Insurance,** As you may recall from above, there are different insurance policies that depends on the type of the services or materials needed. Insurance technique helps spread risks that are too large for any one party bear, and a vast pool of policyholders pays premiums.

  In the contracts, one party may require another to take out and maintain insurance. The project owner requires it from contractors and contractors require it from sub-contractors.

One major concern regarding adequacy of the insurance is; does it covers the right risk? Is the coverage limit high enough, and is the insurance company stable, creditworthy and properly licensed?

- **The Role of Indemnification,** Indemnification (and hold harmless) is a promise by one party to pay certain costs that the latter incurs. Normally used when one party is exposed to risk that arises out of other's conduct and it has full control of the business. A good example is found in a franchise agreement, where

  - Franchisee is in control of the business,
  - Because customers see the franchisor's name and trademarks are on the door, it is exposed to the risk of lawsuits.
  - Franchisee indemnifies franchisor and holds harmless.

In practice, the indemnifying party may ask to exclude certain conduct from coverage, and for restrictions on settlement of claims. They may also seek to control the defense of the claim, and want to narrowly limit risks. Whereas the recipients of the indemnification wants it to be broad.

- **The Role of Limitation of Liability,** This is part of action section of the contract and limits the amount of exposure a company faces in the event a lawsuit is filed or another claim is made. As not all types of damages can be covered by insurance, it is important to limit the claims and to cap the amount that can be recovered. Usually there is an exclusion to certain types of damages like; consequential damages repair and replace.

Regarding the damages, there are two types in businesses, "direct damage" directly from a breach, such as the cost to repair or complete the work in the contract, the loss of value of lost or damaged work.

The other type is "consequential damage" like loss of profit or revenue; in most contracts, this is limited as it can lead to enormous losses. Just compare the contractor's cost to complete delayed work (direct damage) to the loss of operating revenue an owner might claim because of late completion.

In practice, both parties' potential liability should be reasonably limited. Most companies prefer to limit their liability to "direct" damages, which are the actual cost of correcting their failure to perform, and exclude exposure to "incidental", or "consequential" damages over which they have no control.

- **The Role of Pledge,** This is done through **security interest, or escrows**, the former is an enforceable legal claim or lien on collateral that has been pledged.

While in the "escrows "technique, the parties deposit cash or other property with a neutral third party, who agrees to release it only in accordance with the terms of the escrow agreement. Both above techniques are used to lessen credit risk or (financial risk).

Practically speaking, they are using a bank guarantee, bond, or standby letter of credit as those give an advantage (i.e. disincentive for the contractor to breach and easily collect cash).

Part- 6 Justice of Contracts

1.6.1 Laws Governing Contracts

In every contract there is a provision or article of "governing law", if the parties are local to one another, national (or provincial law) will govern their agreement.

The governing law article, also known, as a choice of law article, is a declaration that establishes the higher authority, should a dispute arise from a contract or agreement. In its absence, common law conflicts of law principles fill in the void. When drafting, this governing law article may guide the parties to dispute solving an issue. To complement the governing law article, you should include a choice of forum and venue in the governing state, or emirate, or country.

Consider the following factors when choosing a forum [17]

- ❖ Certainty,

    - Does that country's law have a record of accomplishment of dealing with similar cases?
    - Are the results reasonably predictable given similar circumstances?

- ❖ Accessibility

    - How easy is it to determine what the law is regarding disputes!
    - What are the sources of forum's laws (statutes, court cases, scholarly books) and how accessible are those sources?
    - Is the governing law written in a language that both parties can understand?

- ❖ Transparency and Fairness,

    - Does the local law generally handle cases the same way for both foreigners and citizens?
    - How easy is it to change the law?

❖ Neutrality

In drafting the article of governing law, one should draw attention to the language defining the scope of the article. Below you will find an example of how to simplify this issue:

Version	The write up language	Note
Version1	The laws of ….govern all matters with respect to this contract.	*All matters* does not include tort, fraudulent inducement
Version2	The laws of ….govern all matters with respect to this contract including torts & fraudulent inducement.	It takes in the consideration the torts and fraudulent inducement.
Version3	The laws of ….govern all matters relating to (or arising under) this contract.	

It is preferential for the contract owner to have their national body of laws govern, below two examples of the language defining it:

This Contract will be govern solely by the laws of Great Britain; it will not be governed or interpreted under the United Nations Convention on the International Sale of Goods.

This contract will be governed by the laws of the State of New York, without regards to its conflict of laws rules.

In addition to the governing law choice, the venue is the prior agreement for the location of the court system (or other source for dispute resolution, such as arbitration or mediation). Below is a sample of a write up:

Venue for any judicial proceeding under this contract shall be held in the Super Courts of San Francisco, California, USA.

The parties are facing a predicament, as they cannot determine what national or provincial body of law will be used to interpret the contract.

That is typically left to the judge, but it may have a major role in determining the outcome of a dispute.

In addition to the selection of "venue", the forum needs to be discussed and agreed upon. The Parties should consider the followings;

- o   Court vs. Alternative Dispute Resolution.
- o   The Role of Conciliation /Mediation.
- o   Exclusive jurisdiction or non-exclusive jurisdiction.
- o   Transparency and "procedural" fairness.
- o   Competency.
- o   Home- field advantage.

Moreover, if the forum is agreed upon, there may still be other concerns, like;

- o   Is it lawful to select the chosen forum?
- o   Can the selected forum give you an effective and practical remedy?
  - ✓   Who is likely to be the defendant?
  - ✓   Where do they have assets?
  - ✓   Where is the evidence and witnesses?
  - ✓   What is the finality of proceedings?
  - ✓   Do they have experience with this type of dispute?
- o   Forum's reputation for being fair?
- o   Reputation of handling cases quickly.
- o   Cost.

1.6.2 Alternative Dispute Resolution (ADR)

If the parties of a contract disagree, on a certain contract issue, whether it is a financial or technical or employment dispute is created.

A lawsuit is not always the best way to resolve a dispute that is highly technical nature. The dispute may also be resolved by a somewhat less formal procedure called" alternative dispute resolution or [ADR]".

ADR was developed to provide a fordable, faster and more private alternative to litigation.

The focus on ADR was primarily generated from the United State of America. However; it is now a topic of frequent discussion among industry participants around the world. Not surprisingly, acceptance and application of ADR is evolving in different countries and from project to project. A central theme of North American construction law conferences, ADR has also been a central focus for a number of years at international construction law conferences globally. That worldwide attention and growing awareness is resulting in the evolution of various ADR approaches adapted to attempt to avoid, or at least to minimize, the disruptive and costly impact of traditional dispute resolution.

ADR varies somewhat by country and culture. There are significant common elements that justify a main topic, and each country or region's differences should be delegated to sub-pages.

ADR is generally classified into the following approaches: [9]

❖ **Negotiation:**
Participation is voluntary, and there is no third party, that facilitates the resolution process or imposes a resolution. (NB is – a third party like a chaplain, organizational ombudsperson, social worker or a skilled friend that may coach one or both of the parties behind the scene, a process called "helping people help themselves").

❖ **Mediation:**
There is a third party, a mediator, who facilitates the resolution process. They may even suggest a resolution, typically known as a "mediator's proposal", this resolution is not binding.

❖ **Collaborative Law or Collaborative Divorce:**
Each party has an attorney who facilitates the resolution process within specifically contracted terms. The parties reach an agreement with the support of the attorneys, who are trained in the process and mutually agreed experts. No one imposes a resolution on the parties. However, the

process is formalized as part of the litigation and court system. Rather than being an alternative resolution methodology, this is a litigation variant that happens to rely on ADR like attitudes and processes.

❖ Arbitration:

In arbitration, participation is typically voluntary and a third party private judge, imposes a resolution. This often occurs because parties agree that any future dispute will be resolved by arbitration.

Arbitration [10] is a sort of ADR. It is now a common approach to resolution, locally and internationally. It is also part of leading edge focus on approaches to alternative dispute resolution on engineering projects. More and more attention is currently focused on the evolution of special techniques to address the reduction and resolution of disputes. An example of techniques aimed at reducing disputes include "parenting" concepts, dispute review boards, pre-arbitral referees and contractual mediation provisions.

❖ Conciliation:

Conciliation is a less formal arbitration. This process does not require the existence of any prior agreement. Any party can request that the other party to appoint a conciliator. One is preferred but two or three are also acceptable, through all conciliators must act. If one party does not wish to participate, there can be no conciliation.

Parties may submit statements to the conciliator describing the general nature of the dispute and the points being disputed. Each party sends a copy of the statement to the other. The conciliator may request further details, ask to meet, or communicate with the parties orally or in writing. Parties may even submit suggestions for the settlement of the dispute.

When it appears to the conciliators that elements of a settlement exist, they may draw up the terms and send it to the parties for their acceptance. If both the parties sign the settlement document, it is final and binding on both.

Note that in the USA, this process is similar to mediation. However, in India, mediation different from conciliation and is completely informal.

Finally, it is important to realize that conflict resolution is one major goal of all the ADR processes. If a process leads to resolution, it is a dispute resolution process.

1.6.3 Advantages and Disadvantages of ADR:

Advantages and Benefits of ADR:

ADR has been used increasingly alongside and integrated formally into legal systems in order to capitalize on advantages like:

- Suitability for multi-party disputes;
- Flexibility of procedure - the process is determined and controlled by the parties involved;
- Lower costs;
- Less complexity;
- Parties choose neutral third party who is likely an expert in the area of dispute.
- A greater likelihood a speedier settlements;
- Practical solutions tailored to parties' interests and needs (not rights and wants, as they may perceive them);
- Durability of agreements;
- Confidentiality
- The preservation of relationship and reputations.

The flexible nature an ADR means that a tailored solution can be developed. There may even be a 'win-win' scenario, unlike a trial when there can only be a 'winner' and a 'loser'. This brings benefits in terms of maintaining relationships, in family or commercial cases where the parties may need to have continued contact. The adversarial nature of court cases pit parties against each other. The emphasis in ADR is on working together to reach a mutually acceptable solution.

Disadvantages of ADR:

Understanding the disadvantages of alternative dispute resolution can avoid a big mistake if parties would be better served by going to court. The following are major disadvantages:

- **The parties might still go to court.** Unlike litigation its guaranteed result, many alternative dispute resolutions do not offer an absolute ending. You might spend a great deal of time and money but find yourself in litigation anyway.
- **Decisions are often final.** The result, unlike court decisions, cannot be appealed if you are not satisfied. It is up to you to explore various avenues of alternative dispute resolution and consider how binding they will be.
- **Your case might not be a good fit.** Alternative dispute resolutions generally resolve only civil issues or money disputes. These proceedings will not result in injunctive orders for one party to do or cease doing a particular affirmative act.
- **There are limits to the discovery process.** The parties should also be aware that you are generally proceeding without the protections offered in litigation, such as those governing discovery. Courts generally allow a great deal of latitude in the process, which does not happen in an alternative dispute resolution.

Finally, there are cases of pressing legal or economic importance where full-fledged litigation is still the best way to fully resolve a clash of legal rights. Examples include the continuing struggle with the propriety of using affirmative action to remedy discriminatory practices or a subcontracting decision in a union setting that may determine the employer's economic viability. The importance of the issue warrants use of the full legal process, which is best served by full-scale advocacy of opposing viewpoints before an experienced and neutral tribunal.

1.6.4 General View on "ADR":

Implementation of the ADR techniques discussed is logical, given the history of costly, time consuming and disruptive litigation worldwide. Consequently, ADR is recommended especially in the construction and engineering contracts.

For example, in Canada for year 2009, one agency settled 65% of the complaints with ADR, 29% were not settled and 6% of them were unable to be pursued. One of the most used types of ADR is the "arbitration",especially for disputes of technical or engineering nature. It provides an opportunity to bring the dispute before an arbitrator who is already familiar with the subject matter.

An arbitration clause is usually included in engineering & construction contracts (refer to Chapter 2, Part 3 "Claims and Disputes in Construction"). The wording of the clause may indicate that arbitration is mandatory, the parties must submit disputes and they may not proceed by way of lawsuit. An example of a mandatory arbitration clause can be found below;

> All disputes arising of or in connection with this contract; shall be settled under the Rules of Arbitration of the International Chamber of Commerce by one or more arbitrators appointed in accordance with the said Rules.

However, not all arbitration clauses mandatory, they may provide that disputes will be submitted to arbitration if both parties agree. This often just let the parties know about available resolution option.

The country whose law governs the interpretation of the contract, should govern any ADR clause. The ADR act sets out rules about the time and place, the commencement and the exchange of pleadings.

If the parties agreed to a private ADR, the providers should satisfy the following questions:

- What experience does the provider have?

- What specialized education or training does the provider have?
- Does the provider follow any rules of conduct or ethical standards?
- What is the basis for the fees charged?

It depends on the laws of the country as to whether or not private ADR providers have the jurisdiction to award prejudgment and post judgment interest as courts and local governing limits the range of circumstances in which the ADR award can be impeached. So that the court may set aside the award of ADR provider(s) when:

- The case is under a legal incapacity.
- The contract is invalid, or has ceased to exist.
- The award is beyond the scope of work.
- The application was not treated equally and fairly.
- The procedure of ARD did not comply with the statute.
- The private provider(s) committed a corrupt or fraudulent act or there is a reasonable apprehension of bias.
- The award was obtained by fraud.

For example Dubai law No.6 of 1997 § 36; does not allow the Government of Dubai or any of its Departments to agree to contracts that ;[17] [18]

- Have arbitration outside Dubai.
- Have any dispute concerning arbitration, including procedures related thereto, to be subject to any laws or principles contrary to the laws and principles observed in the Emirate of Dubai.
- Any provision to the contrary shall be deemed void and not binding.

I strongly recommend ADR. It is one of the key instruments to resolve disputes amicably and enhance investor confidence in the economy. I have come across a case where in my previous employer settled one of the major dispute over cancelled project. The contractor had imported heavy equipment and machinery like major turbines and generators using ADR, the contractor was compensated with awarded projects, which both parties agreed.

Fortunately and due to the internet, ADR is increasingly conducted online. Online dispute resolution or (ODR, is mostly a buzzword and an attempt to create a distinctive product). It should be noted, that ODR services can be provided by government entities, and as such may be part of the litigation process. Moreover, ADR can be provided on a global scale, where no effective domestic remedies are available to disputing parties.

1.6.5 Major Arbitration Bodies :[18]

- ICC (International Chamber of Commerce) headquartered in Paris.
- LCIA (London Court International Arbitration) headquartered in London.
- DIFC-LCIA (a joint venture between Dubai International Financial Centre and LCIA) headquartered in Dubai.
- DIAC (Dubai International Arbitration Centre) based in Dubai Chamber of Commerce.
- ADCCAC (Abu Dhabi Chamber of Commerce Conciliation and Arbitration Center) based in Abu Dhabi.
- Tahkeem (Sharjah International Trade Arbitration Centre)

The **ICC** recommends that the parties of a contract stipulate the following in the arbitration article;

- The law governing the contract.
- The number of arbitrations.
- The place of arbitration,
- The language of the arbitration

A complete article or clause of Arbitration would read like this:

Any dispute arising out of or relating to this contract or agreement will be settled by arbitration. The following rules apply to arbitration: (i) the current International Chamber of Commerce rules (ICC rules) will govern. (ii) The language of arbitration will be English. (iii) there will be one independent arbitrator selected in accordance with the ICC rules; (iv) the place of arbitration will be Paris, France; (v) The arbitrator shall not be empowered to award damages in excess of compensatory damages, and each party hereby irrevocably waives any right to recover such damages; (vi) as a primary goal of this arbitration is to conclude disputes in a speedy manner at substantially less cost to the parties than litigation, the arbitrator is therefore to conduct the proceedings in a speedy and expeditious manner, each party is limited to presenting two days of evidence including up to three live witnesses, and the arbitrator shall issue an award within seven days after the last hearing date; and (vii) the arbitrator's decision will be final and binding and judgment upon the award rendered by the arbitrator may be entered by any court having jurisdiction.

The following statements are copied from Article 8 of the **ICC** Rules:

- *The disputes shall be decided by a sole arbitrator or by three arbitrators.*
- *Where the parties have not agreed upon the number of arbitrators, the court shall appoint a sole arbitrator, save where it appears to the court that the dispute is such as to warrant the appointment of three arbitrators. In such case, the claimant shall nominate an arbitrator within a period of 15 days from the receipt of the notification of the decision of the court, and the respondent shall nominate an arbitrator within a period of 15 days from the receipt of the notification of the nomination made by the claimant.*
- *Where the dispute is to be referred to three arbitrators, each party shall nominate in the Request and the Answer, respectively, one arbitrator for confirmation. If a party fails to nominate an arbitrator, the Court shall make the appointment. The third arbitrator, who will act as chairperson of the Arbitral Tribunal, shall be appointed by the court, unless the parties have agreed upon another procedure for such appointment, in which case the nomination will be subject to*

confirmation pursuant to Article 9. Should such procedure not result in a nomination within the time limit fixed by the parties or the court, the court shall appoint the third arbitrator.

Regarding the Arbitration cost allocation there are two options;

- o In the event of legal action arising from, or related to, the terms of the contract or agreement, the prevailing party may recover all of his, her or its actual attorneys' fees and costs incurred in connection with the action, unless the applicable tribunal hearing the matter specifically finds that the fees were grossly unreasonable in amount.
- o Each party must bear its own costs of resolving any dispute under this contract or agreement.

1.6.6 International Law

It is important to highlight the Convention on contracts for the International Sale of Goods. This law may be applied for the sale of goods between two different countries; it does not apply to the sale of services, electricity or any non-sales contracts. There are many countries not included in the UN's treaty so the Convention is not relevant.

Part- 7 Contracts Administration (CA)

1.7.1 Introduction

After awarding the contract, the client must appoint a contract administrator to be responsible for performance in accordance with the terms and conditions.

The contract administrators will develop, negotiate and evaluate the contract on behalf of the client. They are charged with ensuring that both parties are complicit with the terms and conditions, as well as ensuring that the contract abides by provincial and federal laws.

Contract administrators: review plans, specifications and contracts to ensure the correct equipment is obtained, and order material and subcontractor services.

1.7.2 Contract Administration Responsibilities;

Usually, the client appoints a contract administrator or a contract administration team to carry out these functions. The team or individual will only carry out the duties specifically delegated to them. In large projects, a project team that supervises day-to-day activities of the contractor may assist the contract administrator or administration team. The following are contract administration responsibilities;

- See to timely contract performance in accordance with the specifications and provisions, while maintaining the quality and legal rights of parties.
- Ensure that all deadlines and requirement for payments and shipping are met.
- Processing requests for information, variations, disputes, claims, notices of termination and contract cancellations in accordance with terms and conditions.
- Maintain complete documentation of contract performance or non-performance to protect the client's rights.

- Establish the specific target date of completion if the contract period is stated in a number of calendar days.
- Analyze potential risks involved with specific terms.
- Stay up to-date with legislative changes and coordinate with the legal department as needed.
- Ensure that employees understand and comply with all terms and conditions.
- All other preliminary actions needed to facilitate performance by the contractor.

1.7.3 Contract Administration Tasks

To achieve qualified performance and successful contract scheduling the contract administration has to look after the following tasks:

1.7.3.1 Become Familiar with Contract (Post-Award Conference);

A conference is to be held with the awarded contractor and the client's team including the contract administrator so that;

- Both parties may achieve a clear, mutual understanding of the requirements.
- A partnering concept is instituted via mutual respect for each other.
- Mutual goals may be established.
- Effective lines of communication between both parties are established.
- Potential problems can be identified up front.

1.7.3.2 Host Implementation meetings (Correspondences with Contractors)

Before the contract performance begins, the contractor shall be notified in writing that:
- Not changes should be made to the contract terms, conditions, and specifications without written authorization signed by the authorized concerned contract administrator.

- The concerned contract administrator is authorized to sign general correspondence documents such as memos, clarifications on technical matters, variation to work and more.
- The concerned contract administrator, in coordination with the supporting project team will prepare correspondences on finance, legal matters, those involving scope of work, or claims affecting costs.
- All correspondences with the contractor must be in writing, other than routine coordination with contract personnel.
- In the event that the contractor identifies ambiguities or deficiencies in the contract terms or specifications, they can submit a request for information, the concerned contract administrator will review, process and clarify to avoid unnecessary delays.

1.7.3.3 Develop Project Schedules (Performance and Delivery Schedules)

To ensure the timeliness of delivery or completion of the works and services, the contract administrator or team should;

- Ensure that the schedules, particularly for lengthy and complicated projects, are accurate, comprehensive and realistic.
- Identify as early as possible, and draw up alternative or preventive measures for risk to the timeliness of the delivery or performance.
- Regularly compare actual progress, as reported by the project support team, against schedules to identify and immediately implement corrective actions when needed.
- Ensure that the quantity of materials or works delivered or performed are within the allowed tolerances.
- If the quantity exceeds the allowed tolerance, the contract administrator or team must prepare a written report clearly explaining and describing the excess deliveries, giving recommendations, including justifications, based on the contract terms and conditions.
- Obtain the contract owner's decision on what to do with the excess items delivered.

1.7.3.4 Establish Proper Documentation and Payment Process (Cost Control)

The contract administrator or team shall examine and validate all costs claimed by the contractor. This examination is more hassle with the cost-plus contract type.

During contract or agreement, or purchase order performance or delivery changes to the contract terms, conditions and specifications may be needed. These changes are known as variations, and may be implemented in two forms;

Bilateral variations are when the two parties of the contract reach mutual agreement on changes to be implemented, including the equitable adjustment for changes.

To maintain harmonious relationships with contractors / suppliers, the client and their supply management and the contract administrator should exert all efforts to implement changes to contracts, purchase orders terms, specifications and conditions through a bilateral agreement. As opposed to resorting to unilateral change orders.

To implement bilateral variation, the contract administrator or team shall obtain estimates for the cost of the changes prior to the receipt of the contractor / supplier's proposal. The client, and supply management, and the contract administrator or team will conduct negotiations related to the cost, time, and other issues in order to finalize budget availability. All involved then prepare a report in order to start processing the issuance of a formal variation order, following standard policies and delegations.

Unilateral Variations, occur if a mutual agreement on the changes cannot be reached, then the client with the help of the supply management and contract administrator will enforce their rights to unilaterally order changes. These are to be implemented through the variation order as per the variations article or clause in the contract or purchase order.

The contractor or supplier is obliged to proceed with the change upon receipt of the signed variation order.

1.7.3.5 Processing Variation Orders

A variation order should, at minimum, should contain the following;

- The title of the contract including the contract number or purchase order number.
- Names of the parties involved.
- Variation order number and its effective date.
- A definitive statement of work being varied, added or deleted,
- A detailed description of changes to the items, specifications, terms and conditions or completion date.
- Attachments of drawings, sketches, and other technical descriptions
- The value of the work or materials and the related changes to be implemented.
- Commencement and expected completion or delivery dates.
- Justifications for why the changes have to be implemented, their financial impact and effect on the performance and delivery.

After each variation, the contract administrator or team shall distribute copies to the concerned contractor or supplier. They will also follow up with the performance, payment and adjustment of insurance policies and related contract securities.

You can refer to Chapter 3, Attachment 5 for a sample variation order form.

1.7.3.6 Acceptance of the Works with Required Quality

This is one of the main tasks of the contract administrator or team. Formal acceptance constitutes acknowledgment that the work and materials delivered by the contractor conform to the quality stipulated, specifications, quantity and other requirements set forth in the contract.

Contractors should present the completed work or services for acceptance in accordance with the contract provisions.

Acceptance of purchased items, will usually be documented by the "Goods Received Note-GRN" while acceptance of the services or works will be documented by Preliminary (or Provisional) Acceptance Certificate (PAC), and at the end of the contract by Final Acceptance Certificate (FAC).

The place of the acceptance will be stipulated in the contract. For items inspected at the source, inspection will not be done for acceptance purposes when the items reach the destination, but be made for possible damages or substitution in transit or fraud.

Acceptance may be revoked if,

- There is non-conformance and it was not rectified within a reasonable period.
- Non-conformance was not discovered before acceptance and the non-discovery was because of;
  ✓ Difficulty by nature.
  ✓ The contractor's assurances.

Revocation should be done within a reasonable period from the discovery of non-conformance and before any substantial changes in the performance.

1.7.3.7 Managing Claims and Disputes

During contract period and in the work performance phase, claims are created on issues, which are mostly related to the encountered conditions or events. However, the basis of claim and the essential for development are contained in the contract documentation and the information supplied or not supplied in tendering stage.

If both parties agree, the raised matter then is then considered, as "Claim" if there is no agreement it is a dispute.

Most claims are a management issue taken on by the contract administrator or team. The process needs efficient and effective management during the entire life cycle of the contract.

There are two types of claims:

Contractual Claim, These are claims based on the terms and conditions of the contract.

Non-contractual Claim, These are requests for ex-gratia or sympathy for damages or losses suffered by the contractor, for which the concerned contract administrator or team cannot be obliged to pay. Most likely, non-contractual claims will be rejected; there may be cases where they merit some consideration because of exceptional circumstances.

All claims should be reviewed, processed, and settled within the period specified in the contract. It in the absence of a specified period, settlement should be reached within a reasonable period from the event-giving rise to the claim.

All payments must be made completed for accepted works or delivered materials as stipulated in the scope of the works of the contract.

Partial payments are to be made in the following circumstances;

- The contract provides that progress payments are to be made based on the work completed by the contractor.
- The contract provides for partial reimbursements in cost-reimbursement.
- Part of the payment is to be withheld for retention or other purposes.

In addition, payments may be withheld in part or in full in the following situations;

- When the contract provides for retention.

- The contractor has previously overpaid or owes the client) money because of his actions or inactions.
- Because of judicial action or applicable law involving the contractor, parties other than the contractor have made claims against client.

Refer to Chapter 2, Part 3 "Claims and Dispute in Construction" for more information about construction.

1.7.3.8 Termination /Contractor Performance Evaluation /Close out Contract.

1.7.3.8.1 Termination of the Contract

When the quality of the work or materials is not qualified, the contract may be fully or partially terminated at the convenience of the client due to the documentation and reporting of the contract administrator or team.

A contract may be terminated for the following reasons:

- The contractor abandons the work or fails to make progress to a degree that acceptable performance is endangered.
- The contractor fails to commence or complete any work/materials requirement within the time specified.
- The contractor fails to perform any other contract provision.
- The contractor fails to give adequate assurances.
- Non-performance can be reasonably anticipated because of certain situations and termination is in the best interest of the concerned client.

If the termination is decided on, the contract administrator or team must prepare a written termination notice that should state the following;

- Type of termination.
- Contract article authorizing the termination.
- Effective date of termination.
- Extent of terminated work or service.

- Any portion of the uncompleted work to be continued, in case of a partial termination,
- Any other special instructions to the contractor.

It is professional and a good practice, that before termination is made, the contract administrator or team must carried out the followings;

- **Demand for Adequate Assurance**; when a contractor fails to make satisfactory progress to a degree that performance is endangered, or there is some other failure that is cause for concern, a written demand should be issued. This will specify and normally give the contractor a certain period to assure the client and contract administration that action will be initiated to rectify the failure.

There is no need for a demand if the contractor positively states through words or actions that they will not or cannot perform the contractual obligations.

- **Notice of Impending Termination;** if the contractor continues to fail to perform in accordance with the contract's terms, the contractor will be advised in writing of the possibility of termination. This notice will:
  - ✓ Define the specific acts or failures to act, that have led to this tentative conclusion.
  - ✓ Call the contractor's attention to its liabilities in the event that the contract is terminated for default.
  - ✓ Request the contractor to show reason why the contract should not be terminated for default.
  - ✓ State that failure of the contractor to explain why the contract should not be terminated. This may be taken as an admission that no valid explanation exists.
  - ✓ When appropriate, invite the contractor to clarify the matter at a conference.
  - ✓ Advise the contractor that failure to respond within a reasonable period may result in an immediate termination for cause.

1.7.3.8.2 Contractor Performance Evaluation

The contract administrator or team should prepare a written evaluation of the contractor's performance. This evaluation is conducted following the completion or termination of the contract, such evaluation is retained and filed which enhances the commercial register of the client.

The written evaluation report should contain adequate information on the following;

- Quality of materials and workmanship.
- Timely completion.
- Compliance with contract requirements.
- Degree of supervision required during performance.
- Safety records.
- Timely and accurate submission of invoices.
- Tendencies to submit inflated claims for extra payment, (if any).

A performance evaluation or review enables contractors and clients to assess and evaluate in a standardized manner. This ensures that the best contractors get work, while the poor performers are held responsible.

It is important that performance reviews are as objective as possible. The scoring system must stay largely the same. Contractor's performance reviews are an important part of projects and the industries at large they enable hard and smart working contractors to continue to do good work and improve.

A sample "contractor performance evaluation report" form is in Chapter 3. Attachment no.6

1.7.3.8.3 Close-Out of the Contract

The following have to be accomplished by the contract administrator or team, in coordination with the client before closing out a contract.

- All supplies and/ or services have been completed or delivered in accordance with terms and requirements.
- The contractor has executed a release of claims.
- The contract time of completion has been formally adjusted, if necessary.
- Issues concerning liquidated damages have been resolved.
- Sufficient funds have been withheld from payment to offset liquidated damages, or any other indebtedness of the contractor.
- All contractual obligations during the warranty period, if any, have been completely fulfilled, and the commencement date of the warranties and guarantees or maintenance agreements are established.
- All administrative requirements have been completed and all necessary information to be included in the contract files have been obtained.
- As-build drawings, warranties, guarantees, spare-parts lists, training, instructions, manuals, photographs and other deliverables have been completed as stipulated.
- All adjustments have been made to the contract price except those adjustments that may result from items excepted by the contractor's release of claims.

Practically the contract is closed by issuance of the final acceptance certificate by the client in coordination with the contract administrator or team. This is after ensuring that all the pre-requisites for closing out have been accomplished or verified and that the performance evaluation report has been completed.

CHAPTER -2

CONSTRUCTION CONTRACTS

Part 1 FIDIC Contracts Forms

2.1.1 Introduction

In general, construction contracts are complicated and connected to many subjects like labor, properties, materials, design services, sub-contracting statutory permits legal environmental control,adjudication, safety, financial rules …etc,

Nowadays, most construction works especially those related to major projects use International Federation of Consulting Engineers (FIDIC) copies of contracts. *"Federation International des Ingenieures- Couseils" was* originally founded in Ghent, Belgium in 1913 by the national associations of consulting engineers of Belgium.

FIDIC, has issued several contract books, which are classified according to the types of the works. Most of those books have more than 20 clauses and majority of those clauses are common in several books, such as Green Book, which is a short form contract with 15 clauses covering 10 pages. The civil construction Red Book now has more than 20 clauses.

The followings are the FIDIC's Books, which are used internationally:

- Short Form of Contract 1st Ed (1999 Green Book)

- Construction Contract 2nd Ed (2017 Red Book)
- Plant and Design-Build Contract 2nd Ed (2017 Yellow Book)
- EPC/ Turnkey Contract 2nd Ed (2017 Silver Book)
- Design Build Operate (DBO) Contract (Golden Book)
- Dredging and Reclamation Works 2nd Ed (2016 Blue Book).
- Underground Works, new edition (2019 Emerald Book),.
- Client/Consultant Model Services Contract 5th Ed (2017 White Book).
- Design-Build and Turnkey Contract, 1st Ed. (1995 Orange Book).

FIDIC also published new Red Book-Multi Lateral Development Banks Harmonized Contract (2005 MDB Ed.). It is the Conditions of Contract for Construction for Building and Engineering works designed by the Employer. The following six multi-development banks have participated in the preparation of this book;

- African Development Bank
- Asian Development Bank
- Black Sea Trade and Development Bank
- Caribbean Development Bank
- European Bank for Reconstruction and Development
- Inter-American Development Bank

FIDIC try to develop and strengthen their books' clauses by issuing new editions from time to time. The World Bank has indicated its intention to incorporate the Red Book into its standard bidding documents and to permit the use of the Yellow Book on appropriate projects.

To choose appropriate FIDIC contract form or book, it is necessary that a Promoter /Owner of a project should consider, carefully analyze, and determine the four main aspects that govern the conditions and success of the chosen standard form. These **four** aspects are;

- The allocation of the essential functions found in a construction or engineering project, in particular the design function.
  In construction, there are many main functions and titles like; Promoter, sometimes referred to as the Employer or Owner.

Alternatives include Financier, Designer, Contractor, and Certifier….etc.

- The allocation of the **risk** inherent in the project.
  In construction, risk occurrence has high probability, according to British Std. No 4778, Part 3, section 3.1(1991) [12]. The risk is defined as "A combination of the probability, or frequency of occurrence of a defined hazard and the magnitude of the consequences of the occurrence." Later, the word "hazard" was replaced by more neutral words such as "event", which allow for the possibility of positive or negative consequences.

  The applicable law of contract allocates the risks envisaged in that contract to the contracting parties. It is the function of a standard form of contract to either affirm that location, re-allocate these risks from one to the other contracting party or spread them to third parties.

  If a risk is not allocated to one of the contracting parties either by the applicable law of the contract or by the terms of the contract itself, it would be expected that a court or an arbitrator will ask the following questions when they are required to adjudicate the issues arising;

  ✓ Which party can best foresee the risk?
  ✓ Which party can best control the risk or its consequences?
  ✓ Which party can best bear the risk?
  ✓ Which party most benefits or ultimately suffers if the risk eventuates?

- The allocation of the **management** role.
  The Promoter is the owner of the project and as per FIDIC Red Book should allocate the risk and obligations as per the contract conditions. The Engineer is a designer responsible, (unless otherwise stated) for design, and supervision. Furthermore, the Engineer has role in the adjudication of disputes. The Contractor

is the entity responsible for construction and completion of the project.

- The method of timing of **remuneration** for the contractor.
  In the Yellow and Red Books, the principle of re-measurement is the criteria for payment of the Contractor based on monthly certificates for work executed and accepted. Provisions are also contained for the Employer's right to vary the work and for the valuation of variations and payments for such variations. Besides variations in quantities, rates and prices may also vary because of varied work.

In addition to the above four aspects, the following characteristics and checklist need to be consider identifying which FIDIC form to use;

- ❖ Choice of the type of the project to be procured.
- ❖ Choice of design, and whether, or not it has an exclusive nature.
- ❖ Checking of how and when payment is made.
- ❖ Certainty of final cost of the project.
- ❖ Method of tendering
- ❖ Control during construction.
- ❖ The possibility or probability of having a variation or change in the works after entering into the contract.

Below is a simple comparison between the Red, Yellow, Silver, Green and White Books Forms [12,] of the (design, risk sharing, payment, and supervision) functions;

Form of Contract	Design Function	Risk sharing	Payment	Supervision
Red, 2nd. Ed.	Independent engineer	Balanced	Re-measurement, monthly statements	Engineer
Yellow, 2nd.Ed.	Independent engineer, and Contractor	Balanced	As per progress, and set out in Preamble.	Engineer

Silver, 2nd.Ed.	Contractor	Extensively by Contractor	Lump sum/ schedule of payments	Employer/ Employer's representative
Green, 1st.Ed.	Contractor	Reasonable balance	Various options; Monthly statements	Employer's representative
White 5th.Ed.	Supply of services	High percentage taken by the Employer	Daily and hourly basis or lump sum	Employer

2.1.2 Roles of Employer, Engineer, and Contractor.

In FIDIC contract forms, they drafted clauses to stipulate and organize the roles of the Employers, Contractors, Engineers, and Consultants that help to mitigate any misunderstanding or confusion during the contract period.

In the FIDIC Red Book,2017, clause 2 "**The Employer**" has following sub- clauses 2.1,2.2,2.3,2.4,2.5 and 2.6, covering the following first six roles of the **Employer**; (both sub-clauses 2.5 and 2.6 are new in Red book 2017 in related to 1999 edition);

> 2.1-Right to access to the site.
> 2.2-Assistance (Old title "Permits, Licenses, or Approvals").
> 2.3-Employer's personnel and other Contractors.
> 2.4-Employer's financial arrangements.
> 2.6-Site Data and Items of Reference.
> 2.7-Employer-Supplied Materials and Employer's Equipment.

Below, copied from the FIDIC Red Book, shows the inter-obligations of Employer and Contractor;

"The Contractor may request and the Employer shall, within 28 days after receiving this request, provide reasonable evidence that financial arrangements have been made and are being maintained, which will enable the Employer to pay the part of the Contract Price remaining to be paid at that time (as estimated by the Engineer), in accordance to clause 14 (Contract Price and Payment). If the Employer intend to make any material change to his financial arrangements, **the Employer shall give notice** to the Contractor with detailed particulars. Sub-clause 16.1 provides that if the employer fails to furnish such evidence under 2.4, the Contractor is entitled to suspend the work or terminate the contract under sub-clause 16.1, "Suspension by Contractor"; and sub-clause 16.2 "Termination by Contractor".

In the FIDIC Red Book, 2017, clause 3 "**The Engineer**" has following the sub- clauses 3.1, 3,2, 3,3, 3,4,3.5,3.6,3.7 and 3.8, covering the following eight roles of the **Engineer**; (sub-clauses3.1, 3.3 and 3,8 are new in Red Book,2017);

3.1-The Engineer.
3.2-The Engineer's Duties and Authorities.
3.3-The Engineer's Representative.
3.4-Delegation by the Engineer
3.5-Engineer's Instructions.
    o   This is quite different in the various books as it refers to design.
3.6-Replacement of the Engineer.
3.7-Agreement or Determination.
3.8-Meetings.

Clause 3.7 "Agreement or Determination", provides "The Engineer shall consult with both parties jointly and/or separately, and shall encourage discussion between the parties in an endeavor to reach agreement. The Engineer shall commence such consultation promptly to allow adequate time to comply with the time limit for agreement under Sub-Clause 3.7.3 [Time limits]. Unless otherwise proposed by the Engineer and agreed by both Parties, the Engineer shall provide both parties with a record of the consultation"

In the FIDIC Red Book, 2017, clause 4 "**The Contractor**", has the following 23 sub-clauses (sub-clauses 4.4 and 4.5 are new in the 2017 edition, whereas sub-clauses "Subcontractors' and "Assignment of Benefits of Subcontractors" were removed:

4.1 Contractor's general Obligations.	4.12 Unforeseeable Physical Conditions.
4.2 Performance Security.	4.13 Right of Way and facilities.
4.3 Contractor's Representative.	4.14 Avoidance of Interference.
4.4 Contractor's Documents.	4.15 Access Route.
4.5 Training.	4.16 Transport of goods.
4.6 Co-Operation.	4.17 Contractor's Equipment.
4.7 Setting Out.	4.18 Protection of Environmental.
4.8 Health and Safety Obligations.	4.19 Temporary Utilities.
4.9 Quality Management and Compliance Verification Systems.	4.20 Progress Reports.
	4.21 Security of the Site.
4.10 Use and Site Data.	4.22 Contractor's Operation on Site.
4.11 Sufficiency of the Accepted Contract Amount.	4.23 Archaeological and Geological findings.

All the above sub-clauses, 4.1 to 4.23 are related to the detailed roles of the Contractor. These mainly state the work is to be completed in accordance with the conditions of the contract, in the stipulated period, and with the required quality and safety procedures.in addition to those 23 sub-clauses,the Contractor has another role in sub-clause 20.1 "Claims".

For information, the Employer takes on the role of the Engineer in the FIDIC Silver Book. In the Yellow and Silver Books, the design function is allocated to the Contractor and not the Engineer, (with reference to sub-clause is 5.1 "General Design Obligations").

2.1.3 Extension of Time (EOT) and Liquidated Damage

There is no constructional contract without an article or clause covering the extension of time and liquidated damages. The regimes for time and damages are essentially the same in Red, Yellow and Silver FIDIC forms although the Silver Book has fewer grounds for extension of time than the others do.

The extension of time in construction is very crucial for the parties of the contract, as the only function of "extension of time" is to relieve a contractor in the delay of liability for liquidated damages. In practice, an extension of time is also the basis for the calculation of a prolongation cost claim. A typical reference that a contractor can claim is covered in sub-clause 2.1 "Right to Access to the Site" which says:

"If the Contractor suffers, delay and/or incurs cost as a result of a failure by the Employer to give any such right or possession within such time, the Contractor shall be entitled subject to Sub-Clause 20.2 "Claims For Payment And /or EOT" to EOT and/or payment of such Cost Plus Profit. However, if and to the extent that the Employer's failure was caused by any error or delay by the Contractor, including an error in, or delay in the submission of, any of the applicable Contractor's Documents, the Contractor shall not be entitled to such EOT and/or Cost Plus Profit".

After receiving this notice, the Engineer shall proceed in accordance with sub-clause 3.7 "Arrangement or Determination" to agree or determine these matters.

However if the Employer's failure was due to the error or delay of the Contractor, then the Contractor shall not be entitled for time extension, cost, or profit.

2.1.4. Extension of Time for Completion

In FIDIC Red Book form, sub-clause 8.5 "Extension of Time for Completion", is an important clause, says:

"The Contractor shall be entitled subject to sub-clause 20.2 [Claims for Payment and/or EOT] to Extension of Time if and to the extent that completion for the purposes of sub-clause 10.1 [Taking Over the Works and Sections] is or will be delayed by any of the following causes:

(a) A Variation (except that there shall be no requirement to comply with sub-clause 20.2 [Claims for Payment and/or EOT].

(b) A cause of delay giving an entitlement to EOT under a sub-clause of these conditions*.

(c) Exceptionally adverse climatic conditions, which for the purpose of these conditions shall mean adverse climatic conditions at the site that are Unforeseeable-having regard to climatic data made available by the Employer under Sub-Clause 2.5 [Site Data and Items of Reference] and/or climatic data published in the Country for the geographical location of the Site;

(d) Unforeseeable shortages in the availability of personnel or goods (or Employer-Supplied Materials, if any) caused by epidemic or governmental actions; or

(e) Any delay, impediment or prevention caused by or attributable to the Employer, the Employer's Personnel, or the Employer's other contractors on the Site.

When determining each EOT under sub-clause 20.2 [Claims for Payment and/or EOT], the Engineer shall review previous determinations under sub-clause 3.7 [Agreement or Determination] and may increase, but shall not decrease, the total EOT".

Moreover there is sub-clause 8.6 [Delays caused by Authorities] which provides as below additional grounds for Extension of Time for Completion;

"If the following conditions apply, namely;

a. The Contractor has diligently followed the procedures laid down by the relevant legally constituted public authorities in the country.

b. These authorities delay or disrupt the Contractor's work, and

c. The delay or disrupt was unforeseeable.

Then this delay or disruption will be considered as a cause of delay under sub-paragraph (b)* of sub-clause 8.5 [Extension of Time for Completion]".

"Unforeseeable" is for the first time, defined as "not reasonably foreseeable by an experienced Contractor by the date for submission of the tender".

This definition appears to have been inserted as foreseeability is used elsewhere namely sub-clause 4.6 [Co-operation], sub-clause 8.5 [Extension of Time for Completion] at (d) above, and sub-clause 8.6 [Delays caused by Authorities].

This additional use of the concept of foreseeability may be considered unfortunate. This is partly because there is always scope of argument as to what is foreseeable. It is also because the test is rarely if ever, applied literally. Most experienced Contractors can foresee almost anything if they put their mind to it. The true test, which is applied by the Arbitrators in practice, is whether the Contractor should not only have foreseen a particular contingency, but should have made some financial or practical allowances for that contingency. If the problem was foreseeable but it would be unreasonable for a Contractor to add to their tender price and/or to take some practical steps to deal with the contingency, then most Arbitrators will support the Contractor's claim.

2.1.5 Delay Damages

In the FIDIC books, the "liquidated "is replaced by "damage" and distinction is made between a penalty and liquidated damages. Clause 8.8 [Delay Damages] which says;

"If the Contractor fails to comply with sub-clause 8.2 [Time for Completion], the Employer shall be entitled subject to sub-clause 20.2 [Claims for Payment and/or EOT] to payment of Delay Damages by the Contractor for this default. Delay Damages shall be the amount stated in the Contract Data, which shall be paid for every day, which shall elapse between the relevant Time for Completion and the relevant Date of Completion of the Works or Section. The total amount due under this sub-clause shall not exceed the maximum amount of Delay Damages (if any) stated in the Contract Data.

These Delay Damages shall be the only damages due from the Contractor for the Contractor's failure to comply with sub-clause 8.2 [Time for Completion], other than in the event of termination under sub-clause

15.2 [Termination for Contractor's Default] before completion of the Works. These Delay Damages shall not relieve the Contractor from the obligation to complete the Works, or from any other duties, obligations or responsibilities, which the Contractor may have under or in connection with the Contract. This sub-clause shall not limit the Contractor's liability for Delay Damages in any case of fraud, gross negligence, deliberate default or reckless misconduct by the Contractor".

Part 2 Risk Spectrum in Construction

2.2.1 Introduction

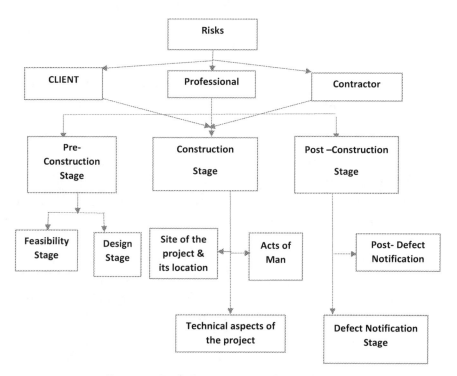

Fig. 2.1- Risk Spectrum in Construction

The above figure [12] summarizes the spectrum of the risks in construction, and the most appropriate chronical classification the risks, which divides the risks into the pre-construction; construction; and post-construction phases. Each of these phases can be sub-divided into further matrices again based on chronology.

The purpose and function of the contract is to allocate the risks between parties. In construction contracts, risk allocation is based on the concept of control of the risk and/or its consequences. Risk management is helpful to mitigate risk occurrence during construction.

We must understand that the risks to which a construction contract is exposed are spread throughout the whole of the conditions of contract. It is not right to relay on the FIDIC Red Book, clause 17 [Care of the Works and Indemnities] which deals with the risks related to loss, damage and / or injury.

This means that the contractual arrangements, the legal rules and applicable law of the contract between the parties and the technical documentation, (including the specifications and drawings), must be clearly and, as far as possible, explicitly stated so that they can be fully understood.

In construction contracts, the duties and the obligations of each party helps to assign the responsibility and liability when risk is allocated. Then the logical sequence that emerges is a flow from Risk to Responsibility to Liability to Indemnity to Insurance.

If the contract cannot allocate the risk, then the responsibility and liability, a dispute arises between the parties to that contract as to whom a particular risk is allocated to. Then an arbitrator or a judge would most likely examine the following criteria (refer to 2.1.1 above) for risk allocation and determine the dispute accordingly;

1. Which party could best foresee that risk?
2. Which party would best control that risk and its associated hazard (s)?
3. Which party would best bear that risk?
4. Which party most benefits or suffers when that risk eventuates?

In spite of using standard contract forms: the contractual arrangements in construction is not easy or spread as shown in below sketch (fig 2.2). However, the allocation of liability is traditionally based on a sharing between the parties involved, in accordance of the provisions of the contract between the Owner (Client or Employer) and the Engineer, as well as the second contract between the Owner (Client or Employer) and main contractor who will certainly have contracts with their own sub- contractors.[12]

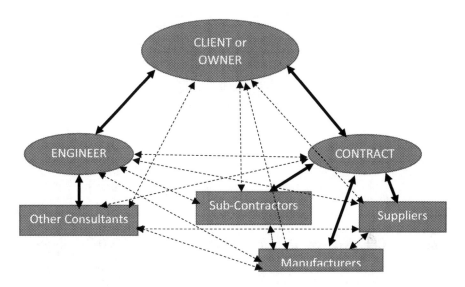

Direct contract ◄──► indirect relationship ------

Fig. 2.2- Contractual arrangements in a construction project.

As stated earlier, the FIDIC Books covers the risks in the two contracts of the Owner (Client or Employer). The following table offers a summary:

Contract	FIDIC FORM /BOOK
Between the Employer and Engineer	The standard form used by FIDIC is the **White Book**, which does not include a provisions reference to a "Risk' topic. It has clauses 16 and 20, which leap to Liability and Insurance.

Between the Employer and Contractor	The standard forms used by FIDIC are the **Red, Yellow, Silver,** and **Multi-Lateral Development Banks Harmonized Books.** The above FIDIC forms deal with risks because of the effects they generate, when they eventuate. The effects can be one of two possibilities, as follows;

The types of generated effects in the Red, Yellow and MDB books are as follows:

a. Related to risks, which could lead to damage, physical loss, or injury, when they eventuate. Examples include- defective design, defective materials, defective workmanship, Acts of God, fire, human errors, and failure to take adequate precautions. These type of risks are covered by insurance.

b. Related to risks, which could lead to economic and/or time loss, when they eventuate. Example include- late possession of the site, delay in receipt of information necessary for timely construction, change in design, and variation to the original contract. Unfortunately, this type of risk not insurable.

Allocation of risk in construction should be based on a sound appraisal of:

1. Control of the risk, its level, and extent.
2. Control of the arrangements made to deal with the consequences, when risks eventuate.
3. Control of any situation connected with the hazard or the event.

As you may recall from chapter 1 Part 5" Allocating Liability and Risks" in order to manage the risks in construction, there should be insurance policies to cover the risks of the Employer and the Contractor.

In the FIDIC, 2017 Yellow and Silver Books, clause 19 [Insurance] has two sub-clauses which explain the insurance requirement and guidelines, as follows (these sub-clauses may differ slightly in Yellow and Silver books)

Sub-clause 19.1 [General Requirements for Insurance].

Sub-clause 19.2 [Insurance to be provided by the Contractor].

FIDIC White Book, "Client Consultant Model Services agreement", Clause 5 [Duty of Care and Exercise of authority] paragraph (i) says:

"The Consultant shall exercise reasonable skill, care and diligence in the performance of his obligations under the Agreement".

Accordingly, the following insurances are required to cover any risk or omission /error that occurred:

- Professional indemnity insurance policy (PIIP).
- Commercial general liability (CGL)

2.2.2 General Requirements for Insurances in Construction

- The terms of any insurance policy shall be consistent with any terms agreed by both parties before the date of the Letter of Acceptance.
- The relevant insurance party shall, within the respective periods stated in the Appendix to Tender submit to the other party: a- Evidence that the insurances required have been effected. b- Copies of insurance policies.
- The insuring party shall submit evidence that the premium of the insurance is paid to the insurance company, as well as give notice to the Engineer with copies of the policies.
- Neither party shall make any material alteration to the terms of any insurance policy without the prior approval of other party.

- The insurance policies shall cover the total period of the contract until the date of issue of the Taking-Over Certificate (Final Completion Certificate) for the works.
- "Works and Contractor's Equipment" insurance policy shall cover all loss and damage from any cause not listed under sub-clause 17.2 [Liability of Care of Works].

Payments by one party to the other party shall be subject to Sub-clause 20.1 [Claims] or Sub-clause 20.2 [Claims for Payment and/or EOT] as applicable.

2.2.3 Force Majeure / Exceptional Events

This clause is found in most contracts, from commercial to construction to various other contract types. It is a very important clause as it considers the risks of certain unforeseeable events, and the affect these events on stakeholders and their ability to perform their job. Mostly, the clause focuses on the following "Classic Force Majeure" events:

- **Acts of God** (fire, flood, earth quake).
- **War, Civil unrest** (civil war, terrorism, undeclared war)
- **Labor Stoppages**.

Moreover, there are other events, known as "Political Force Majeure" events. Some contracts consider them as such:

- **General Change in Law** (tax, environmental, government or administrative action, minimum local ownership requirements may affect fundamental economic underpinnings of the contract).
- **Discriminatory Change in Law** (nationalization/expropriation, denial of permit or consents, and regulatory change specifically targeting one party or a narrow class of parties usually foreigners).

FIDIC Red Book, 1999, has Clause 19 [Force Majeure], in 2nd. Edition 2017 Red Book this was replaced by Clause 18 [Exceptional Events] with same followings sub-clauses.

18.1 Exceptional Events

18.2 Notice of an Exceptional Event

18.3 Duty to Minimize Delay

18.4 Consequences of an Exceptional Event

18.5 Optional Termination

18.6 Release from Performance under the Law.

The Force Majeure or Exceptional Events Clause is a debatable condition, because of sub-clause 18.1, which defines the Exceptional event or circumstances as:

(i)   is beyond a party's control;

(ii) the party could not reasonably have provided against before entering into the contract.

(iii) having arisen, such party could not reasonably have avoided or overcome; and

(iv) is not substantially attributable to the other party.

The same sub-clause 18.1 says:

"An exceptional event may comprise but is not limited to any of the following events or circumstances provided that conditions (i) to (iv) above are satisfied:

(a) war, hostilities (whether war be declared or not), invasion, act of foreign enemies,

(b) rebellion, terrorism, revolution, insurrection, military or usurped power, or civil war,

(c) riot, commotion or disorder by persons other than the Contractor's personnel and other employees of the Contractor and Subcontractors,

(d) strike or lockout not solely involving the Contractor's Personnel and other employees of the Contractor or Subcontractors,

(e) encountering munitions of war, explosive materials, ionizing radiation or contamination by radio-active, except as may be attributable to the Contractor's use of such munitions, explosions, radiation or radio-activity, or

(f) natural catastrophes such as earthquake, tsunami, volcanic activity, hurricane or typhoon".

For example: in respect to above sub-paragraph (f) of clause 18.1, it should be noted that any event of "exceptionally adverse climatic conditions" is excluded from the definition of what constitutes an exceptional event. While this means that, there is no right for either party to suspend the works in the case of an event of "exceptionally adverse climatic conditions", if this type of event has the effect of delaying completion and taking-over of the works or section, the Contractor shall be entitled to EOT under sub-paragraph (c) of clause 8.5 [Extension of Time].

Clause 18 with its sub-clauses explains; (if a party is or will be prevented from performing obligations under the contract),

- Issuance of Notice of an Exceptional Event, when and how many notices.
- Minimizing any delay in the performance by both parties
- Eligibility of giving "Extension of Time-EOT and /or payment for incurred cost to the affecting party".

If the prevention continues for multiple periods and the Force Majeure/ Exceptional Event ceases the works, then:

- Issuance of optional termination and its consequences as per Sub-Clause 16.3 [Contractor's Obligations after Termination].
- The Engineer shall proceed in accordance with sub-clause 3.7" [Determinations] to determine the value of the work done, as well as any other cost or liability, which, in the circumstances, was reasonably incurred by the contractor in the expectation of completing the works. Consequently, the Engineer will issue Interim Payment Certificate (IPC) to the contractor.

If any event or circumstance outside the control of the parties (including but not limited to, Force Majeure/Exceptional Events), arises, which, makes it impossible or unlawful for either or both parties to fulfill its or their contractual obligations or which, under the law governing the contract, entitles the parties to be released from further performance of the contract, then upon notice by either party to the other party of such event:

- The parties shall be discharged from further performance, without prejudice to the rights of either party in respect of any previous breach of the contract, and
- The sum payable by the Employer to the Contractor shall be the same as what would have been payable under sub-clause 18.6 [Release from Performance under the Law].

Part 3 Claims and Disputes in Construction

2.3.1 The Roles of the Engineer in "Claims of Additional or Reduction Payment" in construction

The above subject will be discussed here with reference to the FIDIC Red, Yellow and Silver Books forms of contract. Claims under FIDIC contracts have been an integral part of the risk allocation philosophy and this is clear in the renowned forms. (The philosophy is to allocate the risk to the party best able to control the risk or to cope with it should it arise), this is the basis for the "fair" reputation of FIDIC Red and Yellow Books, although the Silver Book takes a different approach.

The second purpose of the claims clauses is to try to ensure that tender prices do not include large contingency amounts for risks placed on the contractor.

Generally when a claim notice is submitted, it is a normal event and a natural part of the contracting process it should not be taken as the collapsing of relations between the Engineer and the Contractor.

In the new edition of the FIDIC Red Book, the followings are cleared information for claims process:

- The Engineer now acts in the interests of the Employer and no longer has a duty of impartiality. Nevertheless, they have an obligation to be fair when dealing with most claims for payment by the Contractor.
- Employer's claims against the Contractor now have to be made under the terms of the contract.
- Failure by the Contractor to give a 28-day notice is fatal to their claim.
- The Engineer is obliged to respond to a claim within 42 days.
- The Employer may claim an extension of up to two years of Defects Notification Period.

The FIDIC Red Book has an entanglement of clauses governing the roles of the Engineer, such sub-clause 3.2 [Engineer's duty and authority], and sub-clause 3.7 [Agreement or Determination].

Sub-Clause 3.2 [Engineer's duty and authority] states:

"Except as otherwise stated in these Conditions, whenever carrying out duties or exercising authority, specified in or implied by the Contract, the Engineer shall act as a skilled professional and shall be deemed to act for the Employer ".

Sub-Clause 3.7 [Agreement or Determination] states:

"Whenever these conditions provide that the Engineer shall proceed under this sub-clause to agree or determine any matter or claim, the following procedure shall apply:"

3.7.1 [Consultation to reach agreement] states:

"The Engineer shall commence such consultation promptly to allow adequate time to comply with the time limit for agreement under sub-clause 3.7.3 [Time limits]".

3.7.2 [Engineer's Determination] states;

"The Engineer shall make a fair determination of the matter or claim, in accordance with the Contract, taking due regard of all relevant circumstances".

3.7.3 [Time Limit] states;

"The Engineer shall give the Notice of agreement, if agreement is achieved, within 42 days or within such other time limit as may be proposed by the Engineer and agreed by both parties (the "time limit for agreement" in these conditions)".

With reference to FIDIC Red Book, 2017, clause 20 [Employer's and Contractor's Claims], sub-clause 20.1 [Claims], and sub-clause 20.2 [Claims for Payment and/or EOT], I will summarise the source of the claims in construction and the roles of Engineer in claims of both (Employer's claim and Contractor's claim):

Claim	Source/ Reason of the Claims	Sub-Clause. Shall Apply
a	if the Employer considers that the Employer is entitled to any additional payment from the Contractor (or reduction in the Contract Price) and/ or to an extension of the Defects Notification Period (DNP),	Sub-clause 20.2 [Claims for Payment and/or EOT].
b	if the Contractor considers that the Contractor is entitled to any additional payment from the Employer and/or to EOT; or	
c	if either party considers that he/she is entitled to another entitlement or relief against the other party. Such other entitlement or relief may be of any kind whatsoever (including in connection with any certificate, determination, instruction, notice, opinion or valuation of the Engineer) except to the extent that it involves any entitlement referred to in sub-paragraphs (a) and/or (b) above.	Sub-clause 3.7" [Arrangement or Determination].

The followings are the summaries of the roles of the Engineer for processing claims (a) and (b) stated earlier as well as the procedures under sub-clause 20.2.1 until sub-clause 20.2.7.

Under Sub-Clause 20.2.1 [Notice of Claim]:

- The claiming party shall send a notice to the Engineer describing the event-giving rise to the claim (cost impact) within 28days. If they fail to give the notice in this period, then the claiming party has no remedy and the other party shall be discharged from any liabilities in connection to the event-giving rise to the claim.
- If the claiming party falls to give notice of a claim within 28days, consequently the Engineer (within 14days after receiving notice of claim) shall send a notice to the claiming party asking the reasons for this delay in sending the claim notice.

Under Sub-Clause 20.2.2 [Engineer Initial Response]:

- If the Engineer does not give notice within 14 days, the notice of claim shall be deemed valid notice.
- If the other party disagrees with the deemed valid notice, they should send a notice explaining their detailed reasons of disagreement as per sub-clause 20.2.5 [Agreement or Deamination of the Claim].
- Consequently, the Engineer should review such disagreement.
- If the claiming party receives a notice from the Engineer under this sub-clause 20.2.2 and disagrees or considers there are circumstances which led to a delay in their claim notice, then as per sub-clause 20.2.4 [Fully detailed Claim] they shall submit a fully detailed claim explaining their disagreement and the justification and why their notice of claim was delayed.

Under Sub-Clause 20.2.3[Contemporary records]

- Without admitting the Employer's liability, the Engineer can monitor the Contractor's contemporary records during working hours or upon other agreed timing with the Contractor. The Engineer can also instruct /inspect those contemporary records without meaning acceptance or completeness of those records.

Under Sub-Clause 20.2.4 [Fully detailed Claim]

The claim party must submit a fully detailed claim, which must have the followings:

- Detailed description, **contractual and/or legal statement**, contemporary records, and detailed supporting particulars which show the amount of additional/ or reduction in other items as in claims (a) and (b) stated earlier.
- The notice time should be within 84 days of claiming party becoming aware, or at which point they should have become aware of the circumstances giving rise to the claim. The other alternative is within an agreed time between the claiming party and the Engineer.
- If the claiming party does not submit the above **contractual and/or legal statement**, their claiming notice shall be deemed to have lapsed. The Engineer must accordingly give notice to the claiming party that their notice no longer valid within 14days. Now the claiming party can follow up and send justifications for the delay of the concerned statement of concern, including their disagreements. If the Engineer does not give notice, the claiming party notice shall be deemed valid.
- If the other party disagreed with the valid notice of claim, then they must give notice to the Engineer with a detailed disagreement within 14days. Accordingly, the Engineer shall include a review to such disagreement reference with to sub-clause 20.2.5[Agreement or determination of the claim].
- If the event or circumstances giving rise to the claim has a continuing effects, sub-clause 20.2.6 [Claims of continuing effect] shall apply.

Under Sub-Clause 20.2.5 [Agreement or determination of the claim].

- After receiving a fully detailed claim or interim detailed claim (as the case may be), the Engineer shall proceed as per sub-clause 3.7

[Agreement or determination] to agree or determine regarding the submission of either claim (a) or (b).

- If the Engineer has given notice(s) under sub-clause 20.2.2 [Engineer's Initial Response] and /or under sub-clause 20.2.4[Fully detailed Claim], consequently the claim cannot be agreed or determined and all the notice(s) should be reviewed

- The Engineer, after review, will send notice to the claiming party for more particulars/ evidences and shall explain the reasons for requiring them.

- The Engineer will never give any response regarding legal or contract issues.

- The claiming party will send the particulars needed to the Engineer as soon as practicable, consequently the Engineer under sub-clause3.7 [Agreement or determination] will agree or determine regarding either claim (a) or (b) sated earlier.

- The date the Engineer received the requested particulars will be considered the date of commencement of the time limit of agreement under sub-clause 3.7.3 [Time Limits].

Under Sub-clause 20.2.6 [Claims of continuing effect]

- If the event or circumstances giving rise to a claim have a continuing effect, then the fully detailed claim submitted will be considered an interim detailed claim.

- In respect of this first interim fully detailed claim, the Engineer shall give their response on the contractual or other legal basis of the claim, by giving a notice to the claiming party, within the time limit for agreement under sub-clause 3.7.3 [Time Limits].

- The claiming party will submit further interim detailed claims on a monthly interval.

- The claiming party shall submit a final fully detailed claim within 28 days of the end of the effects resulting from the event or circumstance, or within such other period as may be proposed by the claiming party and agreed upon by the Engineer. This final fully detailed claim shall give the total amount regarding claim (a) or (b) stated earlier.

Under Sub-clause 20.2.7 [General Requirements]

- The Engineer, upon receiving a notice of claim and until it is agreed or determined under sub-clause 20.2.5 [Agreement or determination of the Claim],the Engineer shall include in every payment certificate such amounts for any claim as have been reasonably substantiated due to the claiming party under the relevant provision of the Contract.

Under Sub-clause3.7.3 [Time Limits]

- The Engineer shall give the notice of agreement, if agreement is achieved, within 42 days or within such other time limit, as may be proposed by the Engineer and agreed upon by both parties (the "time limit for agreement" in these Conditions).
- A failure to provide information is to be taken into account by the Engineer, especially failures that prevent or prejudice proper investigation of a claim, as it may affect the assessment.

While the claim notice is processing, the Contractor should not stop work and is obliged to continue the work.

In addition, the Employer is obliged to pay the contractor while processing the claim notice.

In the Silver Book contract form, it is intended as a two-party contract, instead of an Engineer there is an Employer's Administration team and the Employer can delegate this team.

2.3.1.1 Contractor's Claims Particulars

The following Table shows the FIDIC's clauses in the Red, Yellow and Silver Books in relation to Contractor's claims and its cost impact results; [13]

Clause (Cl)No.	RED				YELLOW SILVER
	Clause title	Event	Notice	Cost/Profit	

Clause (Cl)No.	RED				YELLOW	SILVER
1.9	Delayed drawings or instructions	Late drawing or instructions	Reasonable prior notice + Cl.20	Cost+ profit	N/A	N/A
2.1	Right of access to the site	Late access or possession	Cl.20	Cost+ profit	✓	✓
4.7	Sitting-out	Error in specified reference points (Not reasonably discovered by experienced contractor)	Cl.20	Cost+ profit	✓	X
4.12	Unforeseeable physical conditions	Adverse Unforeseeable physical conditions	As soon as practicable + Cl.20	Cost	✓	X
4.23	Archaeological & Geological findings	Compliance with instructions	Promptly + Cl.20	Cost	✓	✓
7.4	Testing by the contractor	Instruction for additional passed test, or delay for which employer responsible	Cl.20	Cost+ profit	✓	✓
8,5	Extension of time for completion	Various	Cl.20 (Via 10.1)	Payment/ or EOT	✓	✓ (not weather or shortage)
8.6	Delays caused by Authorities	Delays caused by Authorities	Cl.20 (via 8,5)	Payment/ or EOT	✓	✓
8.10	Consequences of suspension	suspension	Cl.20	Cost	✓	✓
10.2	Taking over of part of the works	Employer used part of the works without Contractor agreement	Cl.20	Cost+ profit	✓	Employer may not take early possession without consent
10.3	Interference with tests on completion	Prevention of test	Cl.20	Cost+ profit	✓	✓

Clause (Cl)No.	RED				YELLOW	SILVER
11.2	Cost of remedying defects	Defects not contractor's responsibility	Notice by Employer + Cl.20	V.O	✓	✓
11.8	Contractor to search	No Contractor's defect found	Cl.20	Cost+ profit	✓	✓
12.4	Omissions	Omission of work	Notice with particulars	Cost incurred anyway	N/A. Claim for delayed tests after completion	N/A. Claim for delayed tests after completion
13.2	Value Engineering	Approved proposal change design	Cl.20, (via Cl13.3.1)	% of net saving	X	X
13.3	Variation procedure	Re-rating justified	Cl.12 +Cl.20	VO	✓	✓
13.6	Adjustment or change in Legislation	Change in law	Cl.20	Cost	✓	✓
15.5	Termination for Employer's convenience.	Employer terminate at will	Cl.16.3 and Cl.16.4	Value of work+ cost	✓	✓
16.1	Suspension by Contractor	Contractor suspends due to Employer's default	May not less than 21days + Cl.20	Cost + profit	✓	✓
16.4	Payment after termination by contractor.	Contractor terminates due to Employer's default	Cl.18.5 and Cl.20	Release performance security + cost (loss or profit and damage)	✓	✓
17.4	Indemnities by Contractor	Loss or damage to works,due to Employer's risk	Promptly Cl. 20	Cost + profit	✓	✓
18.4	Consequences of an exceptional events	Prevented from performing any obligation.	Notice Within 28 days, Cl.20	Cost except natural catastrophes	✓	✓

Clause (Cl)No.	RED				YELLOW	SILVER
18.5	Optional termination payment and release	Prolong prevention	Termination by 7days after notice receipt	Value + cost	✓	✓
19.6	Release from performance under the Law	Impossible,unlawful or released by law	Upon notice	Value + cost	✓	✓
20.1	Claims	Contractor consider himself entitled to EOT or extra payment	Within 28days notice,(84 days for fully detailed claim)	-	✓	✓

2.3.1.2 Employer's Claims Particulars

The following Table shows the FIDIC's clauses in Red, Yellow and Silver Books in relation to the Employer's claims and its deduction impact results;

Clause (Cl)No.	Clause Title	Event	Procedure	Comments
2.6	Employer-supplied materials and employer's equipment.	Contractor take Materials and equipment supplied by Employer	Cl.20, Cl.3.7	Notice not required. Only due amount.
4.2.2	Claims under the performance security	Specified failures (a) to (e)	Claims for the amount the Employer is entitled	Any amount which is received by the Employer under the Performance Security shall be taken into account:
4.19	Temporary Utilities	Amount consumed	Cl.20, Cl.3.7	Notice not required.
7.5	Defects and Rejection	Additional cost for the rejection and retesting	Cl.20.	

115

Clause (Cl)No.	Clause Title	Event	Procedure	Comments
7.6	Remedial work	Contractor fail to comply with remedial instruction	Cl.20	
8.7	Rate of Progress	Revised methods cause employer incur costs	Cl.20	
8.8	Delay Damages	Contractor fails to comply with Time for Completion	Cl.20	
9.4	Failure to pass test on completion	Part of time useless	Retesting, or rejection, or TOC (Cl.3.7)	All sums paid for Part, financing, reducing cost, clearing
11.3	Extension of Defects Notification Period(DNP)	Part of works useless due to defect	Cl.20	Max by 2 years
11.4	Failure to remedy defects	Failure to remedy defect within reasonable time.	Prior reasonable notice of reasonable time	Cost of work by other or reasonable reduction or, for useless works, all sums paid, financing, clearing
11.11	Clearance of site	Non-clearance by the contractor	With 28 days from Completion certificate issue date.	Clear the site at contractor's cost.
15.4	Payment after termination for contractor's defect	Termination by Employer	Cl.20	Claim For any additional cost, delay damage, loss & damages
19.1	General requirements for Insurance	Contractor fails to insure	Cl.20	Deduction of Cost of Insurance premium

Clause (Cl)No.	Clause Title	Event	Procedure	Comments
19.2	Insurance to be provided by the Contractor	Contractor unable to insure	Cl.20	Amount equivalent to commercially reasonable premium
20.1	Claims	After repairing contractor's defect	Cl.20	Employer entitles for extension of defect notice period (DNP)

2.3.2 Dispute Procedure in Construction

I shall summarize the Dispute procedures in construction using FIDIC's, 2017, Red, Yellow and Silver forms of contracts. They each have clause 21 [Dispute and Arbitration], which contains the following sub-clauses ;[13, 14, 15]

21.1 Constitution of DAAB.
21.2 Failure to appoint DAAB members.
21.3 Avoid of dispute.
21.4 Obtaining DAAB's Decision.
    21.4.1 Reference of a dispute to the DAAB.
    21.4.2 The parties obligations after the reference.
    21.4.3 The DAAB's Decision.
    21.4.4 Dissatisfaction with DAAB's Decision.
21.5 Amicable Settlement.
21.6 Arbitration.
21.7 Failure to comply with DAAB's Decision.
21.8 No DAAB in place.

In construction, the Employer, Contractor, and members of DAAB agree and sign the "General Conditions of Dispute Avoidance/Adjudication Agreement (DAA)" in addition to the construction contract signed between the Employer and Contractor. This DAA (or DAAB) agreement have 12 provisions, all to organize the work of the (Dispute Avoidance/

Adjudication Board- DAAB). The DAA agreement is followed with an Annex called "DAAB Procedural Rules", which sets up and manages the work in DAAB, it has 11 Rules.

When there is a disagreement on certain issues belonging to the construction contract that leads to a dispute, disputes shall be decided by DAAB only.

The parties are jointly appointed the members of DAAB within a period stated in the contract/or 28days from receiving the Letter of Acceptance - refer to sub-clause 21.1[Constitution of DAAB].

DAAB, from the contract data will have either; one member (the "sole member") or three qualified and suitable members (the "members"). If the number is not stated and the parties do not agree, then DAAB will have three members. In this case, each party appoints one member and then the parties and the selected members coordinate to select the third member who will act as chairperson.

DAAB's members' appointment, or replacement or termination all by mutual agreement of both parties of the contract.

The DAAB shall be deemed to be constituted on the date that the parties and the sole member or the three members of the DAAB have all signed a DAAB agreement.

The expiry of the appointment of DAAB's members will have either been agreed upon by the parties, will be when the contract is discharged or will be within 28days after DAAB has given its decision on all disputes (whichever is later).

DAAB may be expired either before or on the date of the contract discharge, or on 28 days after given its decision on all disputes refer to sub-clause 21.4[Obtaining DAAB's Decision], which ever it is later.

If the construction contract is terminated, then DAAB shall expire after 28days when; (either decided on all the disputes within 228days from termination or the date that the parties have agreed on all matters "whichever earlier").

Failure of DAAB appointment is very rare, but the following cases may lead to the failure of DAAB appointment:

- If the parties fail to appoint the sole member or any one of the three members of DAAB within the specified / or agreed period.
- The parties failed to agree on appointment to replace a member within 42 days after that replaced member's date of being unable to act.
- If the parties fail to sign the DAAB agreement with any member or replacement with 14days of other party, request to do so.(at the end the appointing entity or official named in contract data should consult all parties and members, solve concerns, let all sign the DAAB agreement, and form DAAB).

FIDIC contract forms always wish the parties to solve any disagreements and avoid disputes. Hence, the parties can jointly make a request in writing to DAAB (informing the Engineer) to assist, make informal discussions and attempt to solve any disagreements. Such assistance and joint requests can be made at any time except when the case is with the Engineer to give a "Determination"

Either party can refer the dispute to DAAB and ask for a decision providing;

1. The case within 42days from the receiving date of "Notice of Dissatisfaction -NOD" upon an Engineer's Determination.
2. The reference states that it is under sub-clause 21.4.1 [Reference of Dispute to DAAB].
3. The subject of the party's reference is a "Dispute".
4. The reference in writing with copies given to the other party and the Engineer.
5. For a DAAB of three members, the receiving date is the date the reference was received by the chairperson of the DAAB.

Any reference of dispute to the DAAB under sub-clause 21.4.1, unless law prohibits it, will deem an interruption of any statute of limitation /or prescription period.

After submitting the "Reference", the parties of the contract should provide all information about the dispute and must continue doing their obligations as per the contract until and unless the contract was abandoned or terminated.

DAAB shall give its decision within 84days from the receiving date or within a certain reasonable period agreed upon by the parties.

DAAB's decision is given providing there is no outstanding invoice of payment to any member of DAAB. When payment is received, the decision is released. Any decision shall state that it is under sub-clause 21.4.3[The DAAB's decision] and in writing, both parties and the Engineer receive copy of the decision.

DAAB's decision under sub-clause 21.4.3[The DAAB's decision] is binding for both parties who shall promptly comply it with regardless of whether a party gives a Notice of Dissatisfaction (NOD) with respect to such a decision under sub-clause 21.4.3. Usually the Employer shall be responsible for the Engineer's compliance with DAAB's decision.

<u>Who can be dissatisfied with DAAB's decision, when, and what are the circumstances to commence the Arbitration?</u>

If either party of the contract is dissatisfied with the DAAB's decision, the party can give NOD to the other party and copies to DAAB and the Engineer within 28days of receiving DAAB's decision. This NOD shall set out the matter in the Dispute and explain the reasons for dissatisfaction.

If after 28days from the receiving DAAB's decision, no NOD is given by either party, then the decision is final and binding for both contract's parties.

If DAAB fails to give a decision within the stipulated period (i.e. 84days), then either party may, within 28days after this period has expired, gives a NOD to the other party as per sub-clause 21.4.4 [Dissatisfaction with DAAB's Decision-paragraphs (a) and (b)].

When can Arbitration commence? It will commence in following circumstances:

1. Either party gives NOD on DAAB's decision in the stipulated period and under sub-clause 21.4.4 [Dissatisfaction with DAAB's decision].
2. As per the statement of the last paragraph of sub-clause 3.7.5 [Dissatisfaction with Engineer's determination].
3. Under sub-clause21.7 [Failure to comply with DAAB's decision], and
4. When sub-clause 21.8 [No DAAB in Place] exists.

If the dissatisfied party is dissatisfied with part(s) of DAAB's decision, then:

This part shall be identified in the NOD. This part and any related parts are all considered severable from the remainder of the decision, and the remainder of the decision shall become final and binding for both parties.

In practice and after giving NOD by one party of the contract and before commencement of Arbitration, the parties shall attempt to settle the dispute amicably, otherwise within 28days from the given date of NOD the Arbitration deserves.

You can refer to previous Chapter 1, Part no.6 "Justice of Contracts" to check Alternative Dispute Resolution and Major Arbitration Bodies.

In construction, if the dispute refers to Arbitration when the DAAB decision has not become final and binding i.e there is NOD from one of the contract parties, then the International Chamber of Commerce (or other body) will settle the dispute under its arbitration's rules. One or three

Arbitrators appointed in accordance with those rules will settle the dispute. They will use the law and language that govern the contract.

The Arbitrators have full power to open up, review, and revise any certification, determination, evaluation, decision, or opinion relevant to the dispute.

The Arbitrators will check whom of the contract parties are helping & facilitating the constitution of DAAB, as that will be taken into consideration on the costs of the Arbitration.

There is no limitation in the Arbitration proceedings for any parties; also, the DAAB decision (if any) shall be admissible, Arbitration can be started before or after completion of the works. The obligations of the Employer, the Contractor and the Engineer are all unaltered because of Arbitration being conducted during the progress of the works.

For awarding, any payment due to the Arbitrators shall be paid without notice or certification.

Sometimes one of the parties in construction will fails to comply with the DAAB's decision (whether it was binding or final and binding). In this case, the other party may, without prejudice to other rights it may have refer the failure itself directly to Arbitration. The Arbitration tribunal consequently gives an order through an expedited procedure, whether by an interim or provisional measure or an award to enforce that DAAB's decision.

If that DAAB's decision was binding but not a final and binding decision, then the interim or provisional measure shall be subject to the express reservations by the parties for the merits of the dispute until final resolved award is given.

Any interim or provisional measure enforcing DAAB's decision, which has not been complied with (whether it was binding or binding and final), may include damages or other relief.

Part 4 Subcontracting in Construction:

2.4.1 Introduction

It is a usual practice in a construction, that the Contractor will appoint and use subcontractors in order to complete their obligations of the contract. I will go through and emphasize the information needed for subcontracting using the FIDIC Red Book form of contract, which has a clause no.5 [Subcontracting] with its following sub-clauses; [13]

5.1 Subcontractors
5.2 Nominated Subcontractors
    5.2.1 Definition of "Nominated Subcontractor".
    5.2.2 Objection to Nomination
    5.2.3 Payments to Nominated Subcontractors.
    5.2.4 Evidence of Payments

In a construction contract, the Contractor shall not completely subcontract the whole work and there is usually a percentage in contract data, which states the percentage of an accepted contract amount for subcontracting.

The Contractor shall obtain the prior consent of the Engineer for all proposed subcontractors except those whose names are written in the contract and the material suppliers.

If the Contractor is required to obtain the Engineer's consent for a subcontractor, the Contractor needs to submit full details about the name, address, kind of works involved and any further information the Engineer may reasonably require. If the Engineer does not send a notice requesting further information or an objection to the proposed subcontractor within 14 days of receiving the submission, then the Engineer shall be deemed to have given their consent.

The Contractor shall give notice to the Engineer not less than 28days from the commencement date of each Subcontractor's work on the site.

For any subcontractor works, the Contractor is responsible for the quality and the progress of the work and the employees of the subcontractor.

In construction, the Contractor shall be under no obligation to employ the subcontractor instructed by the Engineer and whom the Contractor raises a reasonable objection by giving a notice to the Engineer with detailed particulars no later than 14 days from the receiving date of the Engineer's instruction.

According to the FIDIC Red Book contract form, this reasonable objection should be due to one or more of the following (a, b, c) matters :(The contractor shall not employ the urged subcontractor, unless the Employer must indemnify the Contractor for those concerns and its consequences)

a. There are reasons to believe that the subcontractor has no sufficient competency, resources or financial strength.
b. The subcontract does not state that the nominated subcontractor shall indemnify the Contractor against and from any negligence or misuse of goods, subcontractor's agent and employees.
c. The subcontract for the subcontracted works (including design works) does not state that the nominated subcontractor shall;

    i. Undertake to the Contractor such obligation and liabilities and will enable the Contractor to discharge the Contractor's corresponding obligation and liabilities under the contract, and
    ii. Indemnify the Contractor against and from all obligations and liabilities arising under or in connection with the contract and from the consequences of any failure by the subcontractor to perform these obligations or to fulfill these liabilities.

The subcontractor must be paid for the completed works and the Contractor has to inform the Engineer for all paid amounts to their subcontractors. Sometimes, the Contractor is entitled to withhold the payment to the nominated subcontractor. In this case, they shall write to both the Engineer and the concerned subcontractor stating the reasons for this withholding.

Part 5 Variations in Construction:

2.5.1 Introduction

This subject is very important in construction as most major construction projects have variation until completion. I shall use FIDIC, 2017, Red, Yellow and Silver forms of contracts, which all have Clause 13 [Variations and Adjustments] which contains the following sub-clauses;

13.1 Right to Vary.
13.2 Value Engineering.
13.3 Variation Procedure.
    13.3.1 Variation by Instruction.
    13.3.2 Variation by Request for Proposal.
13.4 Provisional Sums.
13.5 Daywork
13.6 Adjustments for Changes in Laws.
13.7 Adjustment for changes in Cost.

The Engineer may initiate a variation any time before the completion of the works, other than variations due to "Failure to Remedy Defects". Any variation should not include an omission of any work which is either carried by the Employer or by others unless otherwise agreed by the parties.

If the Engineer gives instruction for variation, then the Contractor (if they do not give an immediate notice about the instruction) becomes responsible to perform the variation in time and without delay or any alteration, unless the Contractor promptly gives notice to the Engineer stating with supporting particulars that :

    i.   The varied work was unforeseeable in regard to the scope and nature of the works described in the specifications.
    ii. The goods and materials needed are not available.
    iii. The varied work affected the Contractor's ability to comply with health and environmental protection requirements.

Consequently, after receiving the Contractor's notice, the Engineer must respond by either (cancelling, confirming, or varying the instruction).

Each variation may include the following;

1. Changes in quantities of any item in the scope of work (this issue most likely does not constitute a variation in construction).
2. Changes in the specification of an item of the work.
3. Changes in the level, position, and/or dimensions of any part of the works.
4. Changes in sequence of timing or the term of the contract.
5. Any additional new works associated with needed tests.
6. The omission of any works, unless it is to be carried out by others without the agreement of the parties.

The Contractor, at any time during the contract period, can either submit a written proposal to the Engineer, which will help to accelerate the completion, reducing the cost, increasing the efficiency, or implement any improvements and benefits to the Employer. That proposal shall be at the cost of the Contractor and include all details and particulars needed.

After receiving the Contractor's proposal, the Engineer shall respond within a reasonable time. If the Engineer gives their consent on the proposal with comments or without comments, consequently the Engineer shall then instruct a variation. Sometime the consent will come from the Employer directly.

After getting the consent of the Engineer and the possible instruction of a variation,the Contract shall complete the particulars requested by the Engineer(if any) and start performing the proposal fulfilling all points under sub clause 4.1 [Contractor's General Obligations], this include the following;

• The contractor shall provide all particulars and details concerning this part of work.
• The Contractor's documents shall be according to the specifications and drawings.

- To start the work after the Engineer's notice of no objection.
- The Contractor is fully responsible for ensuring that the work fits the purpose as specified in the contract.
- The contractor shall undertake responsibilities to ensure that the works will comply with the technical standards and laws.
- The Contractor shall submit all as-built drawings, and provide training when needed.

The Engineer uses one of the following procedures to initiate any variation; [13]

2.5.1.1 Variation by Instruction;

The Engineer may instruct a variation by giving written notice to the Contractor stating the changes needed and any other details and particulars.

Within 28days from receiving the Engineer's notice, the Contractor shall submit details, which include:

- The scope of varied work with details of resources and methods adopted, or to be adopted by the Contractor.
- The program and timing needed for execution.
- The cost of the execution for the adjustment of contract price. In case there is an omission of part of the work agreed by the parties, which is carried out by others, then the contractor will calculate any loss or damages incurred to the varied work cost.

The start date of the variation will be from the date of the Contractor' submission to the Engineer. Consequently, any EOT will be calculated accordingly.

The Engineer shall proceed after the Contractor's complete submission is received to agree or determine any needed EOT and adjustment of contract price.

2.5.1.2 Variation by Request for Proposal:

The Engineer may request a proposal before instructing a variation by giving written notice to the Contractor. The Contractor shall respond in a practicable time, by either:

- Submitting a proposal with details as per the above article (Variation by Instruction).; or
- Giving reasons why the Contractor cannot comply as per (i to iii stated earlier in 2.5.1).

If the Engineer gives consent to the proposal, and instructs variation, then the Contractor shall complete/submit any particulars needed in a practicable time and the variation will follow the above (Variation by Instruction) procedure.

If the Engineer does not give their consent to the proposal with or without comments and the Contractor incurred a cost in preparing the proposal then the contractor is entitled to claim for that incurred cost.

During all stages of the proposal and awaiting the Engineer's consent, the Contractor shall not stop working and shall monitor the progress of the work as per the contract requirements.

In construction, they sometime allocate Provisional Sums in order to facilitate and maintain the work progress when an unexpected part of the work, difficulties or urgent work to be done during the contract period. The Provisional Sums may be used in completely or in part. The amount paid of the Provisional Sums should be after the Engineer has given instruction, including the scope of work and the materials to be procured by the Contractor, whether it is bought from Contractor's suppliers, from nominated subcontractor or others.

The Contractor shall submit quotations for the procured materials or services and invoices of the amount paid, plus any overhead costs and profit. The Contractor shall submit to the Engineer for approval and if no response is received from the Engineer within 7 days from the submittal, then the Contractor is entitled to proceed at the Contractor's discretion.

All statements of any Provisional Sums paid are substantiated with invoices, vouchers, and accounts or receipts.

The Engineer shall take all statements amounts to adjust the contract price accordingly.

In some construction contracts, there is a "Day-work" schedule, which is used for minor or incident works. If there is such work, the Engineer may instruct a variation using a Day-work schedule for pricing. The Contractor shall prepare quotations to procure the materials either from the Contractor's suppliers or subcontractors and submit it to the Engineer. Thereafter, the Engineer may instruct the Contractor to accept one of these quotations. If the Engineer does not instruct the Contractor within 7days from the date of receiving the quotations, then the Contractor shall be entitled to accept any of those quotations at the Contractor's discretion.

The Contractor has to submit a statement every day to the Engineer explaining what they did in the previous day. The statement shall be in two copies, one of which is electronic. The statement shall include a full record regarding resources used in the previous day's work.

If the statement copy is correct, the Engineer will sign and return it directly to the Contractor. If the statement is not correct, then the Engineer will proceed according to FIDIC Red Book sub-clause 3.7 [Agreement or Determination] i.e to agree or determine the resources.

Accordingly, in the next statement the Contractor shall submit a priced statement of the agreed resources incorporated with invoices, vouchers, and receipts to substantiate the cost to the Engineer

In such day-work variation, the completion date of the work will be taken to adjust and calculate the completion date of the contract. In addition, the total Provisional Sum (which may include taxes, overhead, and profit) used will be adjusted to the contract price.

During the contract period, laws may change. According to the FIDIC form of contract, if those changes are; (new laws or modifications to existing laws-judicial or official interpretations of laws which effect any licenses or permits approval obtained or to be obtained by the Employer or by the Contractor).

If those changes leads to adjustment in the execution of the work, then consequently the Engineer shall give notice to the Contractor. In addition, the Contractor is entitled to give notice to the Engineer.

If those changes cause a delay or extra cost for the Contractor, then the Contractor is entitled to claim for EOT and payment.

If there is a decrease in the cost due to those changes, then the Employer is entitled to claim for cost reductions.

Thereafter the Engineer shall instruct a variation and the procedure either through; [Variation by Instruction] or [Variation by request for proposal].

To finalize this article of "Variation" there is one more subject, which is [Adjustment for Changes in Cost]. This takes into consideration when there is a recession or inflation in the market, which causes rises or falls in the cost of the labors, goods and other inputs to the construction works.

The contract will have schedules of cost indexation, the adjustment to be applied to the amount payable to the Contractor using the current cost index. If this is not available, the Engineer shall use a provisional index for issuance of interim payment certificates. When the current cost index becomes available, the adjustment shall be calculated accordingly.

This cost index adjustment method is not used if the contract items prices are based on current prices or current costs.

As noted from above,I explained ; (The roles of Employer, Contractor, and Engineer, Extension of time, and liquidated damages, Extension of time for completion (EOT), Delay damages, Risk spectrum in construction, Insurance requirements, Exceptional events, Claims and disputes,

Subcontracting and finally the Variation), I feel these are important in creating good guidelines for construction contract drafting. I used FIDIC''s forms of contracts. For a reminder, Employer under the Silver Book replaces Engineer.

Attachment no.7 in the next Chapter will have a complete sample of a constructional contract. It is a sample one can modify, as per the case and circumstances, but at the end, the contract's parties have to agree on all its provisions and conditions.

CHAPTER -3

ATTACHEMENTS

Attachment No 1: Form of Agreement between Client and Contractor

---

FORM OF AGREEMENT

THIS AGREEMENT is dated...*Enter the date*..........and made in......
Enter the name of the location...........................

BETWEEN FOLLOWING PARTIES

(1){...*Enter the full name of the client*............} (The "**CLIENT**"),
located address...*Enter the address*................,

AND

(2){...*Enter name of the contractor firm...*} (The "**CONTRACTOR**"),
located address *Enter the address*................,
....

WHEREAS,

1. CLIENT desires to have CONTRACTOR provide qualified and
    experienced personnel to carry out specialized ......*Enter the type of*
    the.................SERVICES, as described and set forth, herein;
2. CONTRACTOR represents that they have the experience, capability,
    and qualified personnel to perform the specified SERVICES.

NOW, THEREFORE, IN CONSIDERATION OF THE MUTUAL COVENANTS HEREIN CONTAINED, AND THE CONTRACTOR's QUOTATION DATED......, IS HEREBY AGREED AND DECLARED BY AND BETWEEN THE PARTIES HERETO AS FOLLOWS:

1- The Client hereby agrees to engage the Contractor to provide the following services (...*Enter the type of* services....), the services will also include any other tasks which the parties may agree on.

2- Contractor, shall exercise all reasonable skill, care, and diligence in the discharge of their obligations, and shall indemnify and hold the client harmless against any claims, damages and loses, which may be incurred by the client as a result of Contractor's gross negligence, willful misconduct, infringement of any valid patent or copyright disclosure of information obtained by them during the performance of this Agreement.

3- The term of this Agreement will Start on.......*Enter the date,.* and Complete on ...*Enter the date.*

4- The Contractor will charge the Client a flat fee of $.*enter the figure.......* (*Write the amount...*only) for the services. Any sales tax and duties required by law will be charged to the Client in addition to the above amount.

5- The parties acknowledge that this Agreement is non-exclusive and that either party will be free, during and after the term, to engage or contract with third parties for the provision of services similar to the above Services provided.

6- This Agreement will be governed by, and construed under the laws of the Province of *Enter location/Province name...*or Territory of *Enter the territory name...*

7- The Client may also at their absolute discretion terminate this Agreement. In such event of termination, Client shall pay to Contractor for the work already performed up to termination.

IN WITNESS WHEREOF, THE PARTIES HERETO HAVE ENTERED INTO THIS AGREEMENT AS OF THE DATE ABOVE

WRITTEN AND HAVE DULY AFFIXED THEIR SIGNATURES UNDER HAND AND SEAL ON THIS …*Enter the number*……..
DAY of…*Enter the month and year…*

_____ (CLIENT)

_____ (CONTRACTOR)

Attachment No 2: Form of Tender Security or (Bid Bond):
Below the wording of Tender Security Bank Guarantee, (*to be typed on original head letter of the Guarantor/Bank*)

Guarantee No; enter the guarantee reference number
The Guarantor: enter the name and address of the bank, unless indicated on the letterhead.
Tender (RFP) Title / Tender(RFP) No; enter the name and number of the tender
To:

The Beneficiary (the "**EMPLOYER**"); enter the name and address of the Beneficiary.

We, the undersigned, enter the name of the bank whose registered office is at _____enter the address_____ have the honour to inform you that we irrevocably and unconditionally guarantee Messrs: [enter Bidder's Name]_____ to the amount of $._enter the figure_ (__write the amount_____ only) against your Invitation to RFP No. _____, for [enter tender title_____],in [enter the location/City/province], dated [*TYPE RFP Invitation FAX and Date here*] _____.

We undertake to pay you the said amount or part thereof at your first demand without warning, any restriction, condition, and without recourse and notwithstanding any objection from the said Messrs: [TYPE Bidder's Name here] _____.

This guarantee shall remain valid for a period of [enter the no of days (xxx) days] starting from [enter Bid Submission Date here] _____ being the date fixed for the submission of Tenders and all requirements for payment shall be received by us within the said period.

Signed and sealed this _____ day of _____20xx__

For and behalf of

_____
Authorised Signature and Stamp of Bank

Attachment No 3; Form of Performance Bank Guarantee (Performance Security)

Below the wording of Performance Bank Guarantee, (*to be typed on original head letter of the Guarantor/Bank*)

Guarantee No; enter the guarantee reference number

The Guarantor: enter the name and address of the bank, unless indicated on the letterhead.

Contract Title / Contract No; enter the name and number of the Contract between the Applicant and the Beneficiary on which the guarantee is based.

The Beneficiary (the "**EMPLOYER**"); enter the name and address of the Beneficiary.

We have informed that …enter the name and address of the Contractor… (the "Applicant") is your Contractor under such Contract, which requires him/her to obtain a Performance Bank Guarantee.

At the request of the Applicant, we…enter name and address of the Bank… hereby irrevocably undertake to pay you, the Beneficiary/EMPLOYER, any sum or sums not exceeding in total …enter in figures and words the maximum amount payable and currency in which it is payable..(the "Guaranteed Amount") upon receipt by us of your demand in writing and your written statement indicating in what respect the Applicant is in a beach of its obligations under the Contract.

We agree that any changes, modifications, additions, or amendments which, may be made to the Contract, or in the work to be performed thereunder, or in the payments to be made on account thereof, or any extensions of the time for performance or other forbearance on the part of either Beneficiary/EMPLOYER or Applicant /CONTRACTOR to the other or any other guarantor of the obligations of either of them, shall not in any way release us from our continuing liability hereunder, and we hereby expressly waive notice to us of any such changes, modifications, additions, amendments, extensions or forbearance.

We further agree that any payment made hereunder shall be made free and clear of and without deductions for or on account of any present or future taxes, levies, imposts, duties, charges, fees, deductions, or withholdings of any nature whatsoever and by whomsoever imposed.

This Performance Bank Guarantee shall come into force on the date hereof and shall continue valid and enforceable until the issue of the Final Acceptance Certificate.

This Performance Bank Guarantee shall be governed by and interpreted under the laws of...enter the Province or Territory laws.

Signed By :
Name;
Date;

Attachment No 4; Form Letter of Tender or State of Compliance
To be typed on head letter of the firm (Bidder)

To:
Enter the name of the Employer
Enter the address of the Employer

TENDER (RFP) NO.   :   Enter Tender number

TENDER (RFP) NAME   :   **Enter Tender Title**

SUBJECT   :   ………..
Gentlemen,

1. Having carefully examined all the Tender Invitation Package(RFP) as per your Invitation Ref. …………dated…../…../20xx.., we, the undersigned, offer to carry out the SERVICES in strict conformity with the said documents within the sum and rates quoted by us as per package (enter the quotation no and date….) attached herewith.

2. We undertake, if our TENDER shall be accepted, to commence and complete the SERVICES at SITE within the time stipulated in Section enter section number as per the RFP….., Annexure 'enter annex number as per the RFP….'-Schedule, attached herewith.

3. 3. If our TENDER shall be accepted, we shall obtain a guarantee from a Bank approved by you, in the sum equivalent to X percent (X%) of the mutually agreed CONTRACT PRICE for the due performance of the Agreement.

4. We agree to abide by this TENDER for a period of [insert Tender Validity Period as per sub-clause ……. of Instructions to Tenderers] from the date fixed for the submission of TENDERS and it shall remain binding upon us and shall be accepted at any time before the expiration of that period.

5. Unless and until a formal AGREEMENT shall be prepared and executed, this TENDER, together with your written acceptance thereof shall constitute a binding contract between us.

6. We understand that you are not bound to accept the lowest or any TENDER, received.

Dated this _____ Day of _____ 20xx _____

Signature _____

Signed by _____

in the capacity of _____

duly authorised to sign TENDERS for and on behalf of:

Messrs. _____

Witness _____

Attachment No 5; Form of Variation Order

CONTRACT VARIATION ORDER (enter contract no)/ VO xx	Check One: ☐New ☐Cancel/Supersede
Original Contract no: Enter contract number	Variation order no: Enter the serial VO number
Original Contract Title :Enter Contract title	

1-Date for Starting and Completing the Original Contract:
Start Date;   /   /20xx   Completion Date: /   / 20xx

2- Specific Description
A-(*Enter the scope of work of the variation*)
B-All other Terms & Conditions of the original Contract (*enter contract no*) shall remain unaltered.

3. Schedule Adjustments:
Adjustments, if any, of work sequence, Critical Milestone Date(s) and, if permitted by the Contract, the Scheduled Completion Date, resulting from (a) this Variation Order, and (b) the cumulative effect, If any, of this Variation Order and previous Orders issued pursuant to this Contract. For Positive/Time extension VOs, consequently the submitted Performance Bond/ Insurance Policies, to be amended (Value/Duration) to cover this VO accordingly.
Adjusted Scheduled Completion Date: *enter the new completion date* (If permitted by the Contract)

4. Variation Order Price:
The full and complete compensation to CONTRATOR or credit to *enter Client name*, if any, resulting from (a) this Variation Order, and (b) cumulative effect, if any, of this Variation Order and previous Variation Orders issued pursuant to this Contract. It includes, but is not limited to, compensation for all applicable taxes, fees, overhead profit, mobilization expenses incurred or to be incurred hereunder.
Variation Order Cost: $ .... ☐Positive ☐Negative ☐No Value
Variation Order Price Remarks: Enter any remarks related to this variation order
(To list all remarks regarding of this VO as per the approval)

Initiated By: *(enter Concerned contract administrator name)* Signature : Printed Name : Date : Title:	
Concurred By: *(enter Concerned project team)* Signature : Date :	**Contract Control Officer** Signature : Date :
Authorized Contract's owner /Employer Signature	**Contractor's Signature**
Signature : Printed Name : Title : Date :	Signature : Printed Name : Title : Date :

Attachment No.6; Form of Contractor Performance Evaluation Report

Contractor Performance Evaluation Report

Service Provider/Contractor Name;		
Contract No;	Start Date;	End Date:
Contract Name/Title;		

Contract Essentials;	Yes	No	
Completed within/on Time Schedule			
Completed within Scope			
Completed within Budget/Cost			
Completed without HSE Incident			
Operational Excellence;	**Excellent**	**Satisfactory**	**Less than Satisfactory**	**Wholly Unsatisfactory**
Methodology/ Execution				
Understanding of Environmental Requirements				
Understanding Site Erosion and Sedimentation Requirements				
Personnel-Suitably skilled/ Qualified/Professional				
Project Organization				
Attitude and Approach				
Levels of Innovation/ Value Engineering				
Lack of scope Creep				
Claims Conscious				
Other Issues; *(if any)*				
Final Recommendation;	**Definitely Yes**	**Probably yes**	**Probably Not**	**Definitely Not**
Would you use the Service Provider again?				

Other Comments; *(add pages if required)*

```



```

Client's Representative Name; .... Signature: **Date:** / /

Attachment No 7; Complete Form of a Construction Contract.

Contract Title ...
Contract No. ....

Contents

Form of Agreement.
Section (A) - Conditions of Contract and Annexes.
A1- General Conditions
A2- Special Conditions.
A3- Appendix to Conditions.
A4- Annexes.
Section (B) - Technical Specifications.
Section (C) - Bill of Quantities/ Pricing Schedules.
Section (D) - Drawings and Attachments.

FORM OF AGREEMENT

THIS AGREEMENT IS ENTERED TO AND MADE IN *enter the city/province/country.* THIS ....…................. DAY OF ....…….............. YEAR TWO THOUSAND ……… BUT **EFFECTIVE** FROM THE .... DAY OF .... YEAR TWO THOUSAND ……..

BY AND BETWEEN

Party one, *Enter the commercial/official name of the Employer,* having its location/ postal address as ....….. (Hereinafter referred to as "**EMPLOYER**", which expression shall, where the context so permits, include its successors-in-interests and assignees) of one part;

AND

Party Two, *Enter the commercial name of the Contractor,* having the location/postal address........................and License no............ dated.......... (Hereinafter referred to as "**CONTRACTOR**" which expression shall, where the context so permits, include its successors-in-interest and assignees) of other part.

WHEREAS
1. The EMPLOYER desires to have certain WORKS performed as hereinafter specified.
2. The CONTRACTOR represents to have the necessary capability, vehicles, equipment, competent personnel and experience to carry out such WORKS and is willing to do so on the terms and conditions hereinafter contained.

NOW, THEREFORE, IN CONSIDERATION OF THE MUTUAL COVENANTS HEREIN CONTAINED, IT IS HEREBY AGREED AND DECLARED BY AND BETWEEN THE PARTIES HERETO AS FOLLOWS:

1. In this AGREEMENT, words and expressions shall have the same meanings as are respectively assigned to them in the Conditions

of the AGREEMENT hereinafter referred to, except where the context otherwise requires.

2. The following documents, which are listed in accordance with their order of priority, shall be deemed to form and be read and construed as part of this AGREEMENT:
   (i) This CONTRACT AGREEMENT.
   (ii) All post Tendering correspondences, which include, but not limited to, the following:
   - EMPLOYER's Letter of Acceptance Ref. No. ...... dated ... and CONTRACTOR's acknowledgement to the Letter of Acceptance dated .....
   - Any clarification letter during evaluation stage.
   (iii) Addenda/Clarifications
   (iv) Special Conditions of the AGREEMENT (Section ...of the RFP Documents)
   (v) General Conditions of the AGREEMENT (Section ... of the RFP Documents)
   (vi) Technical Specifications (Section ....of the Tender Documents)
   (vii) Completed Technical Data Sheets
   (viii) Drawings and Attachment (Section .. of the Tender Documents)
   (ix) Completed Bills of Quantities / Pricing schedules (Priced Part)
   (x) CONTRACTOR'S Offered Bid (Priced and Unpriced) vide covering Letter Ref. .... dated........

11. In consideration of the payments to be made by the EMPLOYER to the CONTRACTOR as hereinafter mentioned, CONTRACTOR hereby covenants with the EMPLOYER to execute and complete the WORKS and remedy any defects therein in conformity in all respects with the provisions of the AGREEMENT within *enter contracted completion date.*

12. The EMPLOYER hereby covenants to pay CONTRACTOR in consideration of the execution and completion of the WORKS and the remedying of defects therein the CONTRACT PRICE of; [17]

The contract price, which excludes value added tax, is:

..../100 dollars	$....

Value added tax (of...... %) payable by the Employer to the Contractor are:

..../100 dollars	$

Total amount payable by the Employer to the Contractor for the construction of the work is:

..../100 dollars	$

These amounts shall subject to adjustments as provided in the contract document.

All amount are in...*enter the currency* funds (*it known currency of the contract*).

IN WITNESS WHEREOF, THE PARTIES HERETO HAVE ENTERED INTO THIS AGREEMENT AS OF THE DAY AND YEAR ABOVE WRITTEN.

Signed and delivered for and on behalf of: Witness;
Enter name of the EMPLOYER.

By :	BY;
Title :	Title;
Date :	Date;

Signed and delivered for and on behalf of: Witness;
Enter name of the CONTRACTOR.

By :	By;
Title :	Title;
Date :	Date;

SECTION (A)

Conditions of CONTRACT and Annexes

A1. General Conditions
A2. Special Conditions
A3. Appendix to Conditions
A4. Annexes

A1. General Conditions

Article 1	⇨	Definitions
Article 2	⇨	Scope of Work
Article 3	⇨	Duration
Article 4	⇨	Co-ordination Procedure
Article 5	⇨	Facilities Provided By EMPLOYER
Article 6	⇨	Contractor's General Obligations
Article 7	⇨	Financial Entitlements
Article 8	⇨	Warranties
Article 9	⇨	Performance Bank Guarantee
Article 10	⇨	Indemnities and Insurances
Article 11	⇨	Taxes and Duties
Article 12	⇨	Variations
Article 13	⇨	Suspension
Article 14	⇨	Termination

A1. GENERAL CONDITIONS

1. **<u>DEFINITIONS</u>**

For the purpose of this Contract, the words and expressions listed hereunder shall have the meanings hereby assigned to them except where the context otherwise requires:

AGREEMENT	Means the Form of AGREEMENT, and these General Conditions, Special Conditions, Annexes 'A' through 'L' together with Section B (Technical Specifications), Section C (Priced Bills of Quantities) and Section D (Drawings and Attachments).
APPENDIX to CONDITIONS	Means the Appendix comprised in this Section which complement, and forming part of, the General and /or Special Conditions.
CONTRACT DOCUMENTS	Consist of those documents starting from the Agreement, Section A, B, C and D and amendments agreed upon between the parties.
CONTRACT PRICE	Means the total aggregate sum to be paid to CONTRACTOR by EMPLOYER according to Article 7 and Article 12 of general conditions.
DAY, Week, Month or Year	Means Gregorian Calendar Day, Week, Month or Year.

EMPLOYER (Client or Job Owner)	Means the person or entity identified as such in the Agreement. The term Employer means the Owner or the Owner's authorized agent or representative as designated to the Contractor in writing, but does not include Consultant.
ENGINEER, or Consultant	Means person or persons, firm, partnership, corporation or combination thereof appointed by EMPLOYER to act on behalf of EMPLOYER for the purpose of the CONTRACT and named in the Appendix to Conditions, or any other competent person appointed by EMPLOYER, and notified in writing to CONTRACTOR, for the purposes of the CONTRACT.
EXCEPTIONAL EVENTS	Means an event or circumstance, which is beyond a party's control, and could not reasonably avoid or overcome it.
FINAL ACCEPTANCE CERTIFICATE, or (Taking-Over Certificate)	Means the certificate signed by EMPLOYER at the end of the warranty period as defined in Article 16 of general conditions.
PARTY (IES)	Means EMPLOYER and/or CONTRACTOR.
PROJECT	Means the Project to which the WORKS apply as described in ANNEX 'A' hereafter "Scope of work".
PROVISIONAL ACCEPTANCE CERTIFICATE, or (Substantial Performance of the work)	Means the certificate signed by EMPLOYER, when CONTRACTOR has successfully completed and handed over the WORKS to EMPLOYER as defined in Article 16.
Release Letter	A letter issued by CONTRACTOR to EMPLOYER after completion certificate confirming no claims and liability against EMPLOYER.

SITE	Means all locations where WORKS are to be performed, and as summarised in the Appendix to Conditions.
SUB-CONTRACTOR(S)	Means any person or persons, firm, partnership, corporation or combination thereof employed by CONTRACTOR for the performance of the WORKS, other than the employees of CONTRACTOR.
Temporary Work	Means temporary supports, structures, facilities, services, and other temporary items, excluding construction equipment, required for the execution of the work, which is not incorporated into scope of work.
Value Added Taxes	Means such sums as shall be levied upon the contract price by the Federal or any Provincial or Territorial Government, and is computed as percentage of the contract price and includes Goods and Services tax. [17]
WORKS	Means all works and activities to be performed by CONTRACTOR under this AGREEMENT.
Working Day	Means a day other than Saturday, Sunday (in some countries Friday, Saturday), Statutory holiday, or statutory vacation day that is observed by the construction industry in the area of the place of work.

2. **SCOPE OF WORK**

The WORKS to be performed under this Contract shall be as specified in the Scope of Work as per ANNEX 'A', which Scope shall be increased or decreased at EMPLOYER's option, and in such case the CONTRACT PRICE and the Schedule shall be adjusted in accordance with the provisions of this AGREEMENT. CONTRACTOR shall perform the WORKS in accordance with the provisions of this AGREEMENT.

3. **DURATION**

3.1 COMING INTO FORCE

The date of coming into force of this Contract shall be the Effective Date first above written in the Contract and it shall remain in force until the issuance by EMPLOYER of the Final Acceptance Certificate. The WORKS shall be completed as per the time schedule stipulated in ANNEX 'I', and maintained thereafter in accordance with the provisions of Article 8 "Warranties".

3.2 DELAY PENALTY FOR LATE COMPLETION

a.   If CONTRACTOR shall fail to complete the WORKS within the time prescribed in ANNEX 'I' then unless such failure is due to Exceptional Event and/or due to EMPLOYER's default, CONTRACTOR shall pay to EMPLOYER a delay penalty for his failure to meet the completion of WORKS as stated in the "Appendix to Conditions".

b.   EMPLOYER shall have the right without prejudice to any other method of recovery to deduct the amount of such penalty from any monies due or which may become due to CONTRACTOR.

c.   The payment or deduction of such penalty shall not relieve CONTRACTOR from his obligations to complete the WORKS or from any of his other obligations and liabilities under this AGREEMENT.

4. **CO-ORDINATION PROCEDURE**

The Co-ordination Procedure defining the practical interface between EMPLOYER and CONTRACTOR is set out in ANNEX 'E'. For the purpose of the PROJECT, CONTRACTOR shall at all times observe the provisions of the said Co-ordination Procedure.

5. <u>FACILITIES PROVIDED BY EMPLOYER</u>

5.1 Services and data to be supplied by EMPLOYER shall be as described in ANNEX" D".

5.2 EMPLOYER shall also supply CONTRACTOR with any other pertinent data and information as EMPLOYER shall deem required for the performance of the WORKS by CONTRACTOR, CONTRACTOR shall take all reasonable steps consistent with his responsibilities hereunder to check the accuracy and correctness of such data and information.

5.3 Upon coming into force of this AGREEMENT, EMPLOYER shall designate in writing its Representative who shall be authorised to act on EMPLOYER's behalf with respect to the AGREEMENT.

6. <u>CONTRACTOR'S GENERAL OBLIGATIONS</u>

6.1 <u>GENERAL</u>

i) CONTRACTOR shall obtain all licenses necessary to enable him to do business in the Country / Province or Territory and any political subdivisions thereof wherein any part of the WORKS shall be performed, and shall give all required notices and shall furnish any bonds, securities, or deposits required by official authorities to permit the performance of the WORKS.

ii) CONTRACTOR shall promptly review the information and/ or data provided by EMPLOYER, including the information contained or referred to in the Annexes, and bring to the attention of EMPLOYER all things which in CONTRACTOR's opinion appear to be deficiencies, omissions, contradictions, or ambiguities in such information and/or data, then if EMPLOYER insists on compliance with its drawings and information, CONTRACTOR shall strictly adhere to them and perform the WORKS accordingly.

iii) Should any works and/or services be required which are not specifically denoted in the Scope of Work, either directly or indirectly, but which EMPLOYER considers being necessary for the proper carrying out of the intent of the AGREEMENT, CONTRACTOR shall furnish all such works and services. Such works and services shall be given at CONTRACTOR's own expense unless he can demonstrate the same to constitute a variation as defined in Article 12 hereafter "Variations".

iv) CONTRACTOR shall, in procuring his needs of goods and services, give preference to sub-contractors and suppliers and such goods and services as are available in the market in a suitable type and quality.

v) The CONTRACTOR shall have the sole responsibility for the design, erection, operation, maintenance, and removal of the temporary work.

vi) The CONTRACTOR shall keep one copy of the current contract, submittals, reports, records of meetings at the site in good order and available to EMPLOYER and ENGINEER.

vii) The CONTRACTOR shall provide shop drawings as required in the contract.

viii) The CONTRACTOR shall include a statement based on the pricing schedule with each payment application.

6.2 PERSONNEL

CONTRACTOR shall provide and employ on the SITE in connection with the execution and maintenance of the WORKS as provided in this AGREEMENT, skilled and experienced supervisors and leading hands as are competent to give proper supervision to the required work they and supervise any semi-skilled labour when necessary.

If EMPLOYER ascertains that an employee of CONTRACTOR or sub-contractor misbehaves or is inefficient or unsuitable about his qualifications or experience, or neglects his obligations or becomes undesirable for any other reason, CONTRACTOR shall immediately evict such person from SITE if required by EMPLOYER, and an acceptable and qualified person shall replace him.

6.3 TEMPORARY OFFICES, SANITARY AND ACCOMMODATION

a. CONTRACTOR shall provide offices and other temporary accommodation for his SITE personnel including sanitary accommodation and, where necessary, canteen facilities. CONTRACTOR shall arrange for accommodation of his own and his sub-contractor's personnel delegated to the SITE. If CONTRACTOR wishes to provide temporary housing and/or camp accommodation for his personnel, he shall submit for prior approval by EMPLOYER, plans of all accommodation he proposes to erect before any construction commences. CONTRACTOR shall be responsible for all costs associated with any temporary housing and/or camp accommodation provided by him.

b. The sanitary accommodation shall be kept in a clean and orderly condition to the approval of the Public Health Authorities and shall be removed on completion of WORKS and all trenches shall be chemically treated and completely backfilled.

6.4 INSPECTION OF THE SITE

CONTRACTOR shall be deemed to have inspected and examined the SITE, its surroundings, and information available in connection therewith and to have satisfied himself so far as shall be practicable as to the form and nature required, the extent and nature of works and materials necessary for the completion of the WORKS, the means of access required, and in general shall be deemed to have obtained all information necessary for carrying out the WORKS.

6.5 CONVENIENCE OF THE PUBLIC

All operations necessary for the execution of the WORKS shall, so far as compliance with the requirements of the Contract permits, be carried out so as not to interfere unnecessarily or improperly with the convenience of the public or the access to, use, and occupation of public or private roads and walkways to, or of, properties, whether in the possession of EMPLOYER or of any other person.

6.6 OTHER CONTRACTORS

CONTRACTOR shall, in accordance with the requirements of EMPLOYER, afford all reasonable opportunities to cooperate with any other contractors employed by EMPLOYER and their workmen and to the workmen of EMPLOYER and of any other duly constituted authorities who shall be employed in the execution on or near the SITE of any work not included in the AGREEMENT or of any contract which EMPLOYER shall enter into in connection with or ancillary to the WORKS.

6.7 AUTHORISED REPRESENTATIVE

Before starting the WORKS, CONTRACTOR shall designate a competent authorised representative acceptable to EMPLOYER to represent and act for CONTRACTOR and shall inform EMPLOYER in writing of the name and address of such representative and the scope of his authority. All notices, determinations, directions, instructions and other communications given to the authorised representative by EMPLOYER shall be deemed to be given to CONTRACTOR.

6.8 FULL RESPONSIBILITY AND CARE

CONTRACTOR shall take full responsibility for the care of the WORKS from the commencement thereof until the date of issue of the PROVISIONAL ACCEPTANCE CERTIFICATE. In case any damage, loss, or injury shall happen to the WORKS or any part thereof, from any cause whatsoever, CONTRACTOR shall, at his own cost, repair and make good the same. Accordingly, at the issue of the PROVISIONAL ACCEPTANCE CERTIFICATE the WORKS shall be in good order, condition and in conformity in every respect with the requirements of the AGREEMENT.

6.9 SAFETY AND SECURITY

    a)   CONTRACTOR shall in executing the WORKS comply with the relevant requirements of the safety regulations of EMPLOYER together with all applicable laws and regulations of Federal or any

Provisional or Territorial Government in connection with the area of the WORK's site.

b) The responsibility for all safety measures required for the WORK rests solely with CONTRACTOR.

c) CONTRACTOR shall, in undertaking 'Hot Works', conduct the same in a safe manner and in compliance with the laws and regulations of Federal or any Provincial or Territorial Government and EMPLOYER's safety regulations, and shall be solely responsible for obtaining all the necessary permits and licenses required by the said laws and regulations.

'Hot Works' shall be defined as those types of work which shall involve the use of open flame, all types of welding and gas cutting of metals, use of apparatus or machines that could produce sparks, and work which otherwise endangers inflammable environment.

6.10 PROTECTION OF SERVICES

a) Any cable, pipeline, or other service exposed by CONTRACTOR shall be protected and supported by CONTRACTOR to prevent damage to the service. Support shall be maintained throughout the whole period of the exposure of services, and it shall be CONTRACTOR's responsibility to ensure that, on and after backfilling or building in, the said services are adequately supported with concrete blocks or other satisfactory means so that no damage shall be caused to them on or after such backfilling or building in. Suitable braces, props, shall support any foundations of existing buildings or roads in, or alongside the excavations or other means throughout CONTRACTOR's operations and, before backfilling, shall be so permanently braced that they shall not be affected by the settlement of backfill.

b) CONTRACTOR shall take all necessary precautions to avoid causing damage to services, including service lines such as cables, pipelines, etc., buried or otherwise, and shall be liable, subject to the provisions of this Contract, to the owners of such services for any damage thereto arising out of or in relation with the performance of the WORKS by CONTRACTOR, his personnel or agents or of his SUB-CONTRACTORS.

6.11 WATER, AIR POLLUTION AND NOISE

a) CONTRACTOR shall, at his expense, provide suitable facilities to prevent the introduction into any sub-surface water bearing strata or reservoirs or other body of water, including the sea, substances or materials that shall pollute the water or be deleterious to life or environment.

b) CONTRACTOR shall perform his WORKS so as not to discharge into the atmosphere, from any source whatsoever, smoke dust or other air contaminants in violation of the applicable laws.

c) CONTRACTOR shall perform the WORKS without unreasonable noise and disturbance, so as not to interfere unnecessarily or improperly with the use or occupation of adjacent properties, whether in the possession of EMPLOYER or of any other party.

6.12 MEDICAL SERVICES, EPIDEMICS AND WORK ACCIDENTS

i) Unless otherwise stated herein, CONTRACTOR shall be responsible for the provision of medical services, including, without limitation, first aid and hospitalisation, for all his personnel employed in the performance of the WORK within the SITE. Such services shall conform to the applicable laws and regulations of Federal or any Provincial or Territorial Government.

ii) EMPLOYER may have medical services at the SITE and may at its option make available such services for the treatment of employees of CONTRACTOR who shall be injured or become ill while engaged in the performance of the WORK. If such services are made available to CONTRACTOR's employees, then, in consideration for the use thereof, CONTRACTOR hereby agrees that:

a. CONTRACTOR shall pay to EMPLOYER the costs of such services.

b. CONTRACTOR shall release, defend, indemnify and save harmless EMPLOYER, its authorised representatives, successors-in-interest or assignees, and all of its officers and employees from and against any claims, demands or liabilities arising from the receipt of such services by CONTRACTOR's employees.

c. Upon the occurrence of any infectious disease at SITE, CONTRACTOR shall immediately inform the competent health authority of the name and address of the patient and shall report the absence or repatriation of the patient due to the infectious disease.

d. CONTRACTOR shall inform EMPLOYER of any accident occurring at SITE or in its vicinity, particularly in the case of death or injuries to persons or damage to property. Such notice shall contain all details and statements of witnesses. Further, CONTRACTOR shall advise the state authorities concerned of such accidents.

6.13 RECORDS AND REPORTS

CONTRACTOR shall maintain a logbook at the SITE for daily recording of the work done and of all events of importance. CONTRACTOR shall submit to EMPLOYER daily, weekly and monthly reports.

6.14 CLEARANCE OF SITE ON COMPLETION

a. Upon completion of WORKS, CONTRACTOR shall, at his expense, provide operational works, including satisfactory disposal of all temporary jobs, construction plant, rubbish, unused materials, and other equipment and materials belonging to him or used in the performance of the WORKS, including the return to EMPLOYER of any salvageable supplies furnished by EMPLOYER but not used. CONTRACTOR shall leave the SITE in a neat, clean, and safe condition. In the event of the CONTRACTOR's failure to comply with the previous, after written notice from EMPLOYER, EMPLOYER shall accomplish the same at CONTRACTOR's expense.

b. CONTRACTOR shall notify forthwith and with dispatch raise and remove any object, which shall sink accidentally in the course of the construction and completion of WORKS or otherwise deal with the same as EMPLOYER shall direct. In the event of CONTRACTOR not carrying out the obligations imposed upon him by this sub-article, EMPLOYER shall buoy and lift such sunken object and remove the same (without prejudice to the right of EMPLOYER to hold CONTRACTOR liable). CONTRACTOR shall refund all costs incurred in addition to that. The fact that the underwater object shall be insured, or declared total loss shall not release the CONTRACTOR from his obligations under the present sub-article to raise or remove the same.

7. **FINANCIAL ENTITLEMENTS**

7.1 CONTRACT PRICE

In consideration of performing the WORKS in full conformity with the AGREEMENT, EMPLOYER shall pay to CONTRACTOR the CONTRACT PRICE as specified in the priced part of Section **C** (the Bills of Quantities/Pricing schedules) in the manner set forth in sub-articles 7.2 and 7.3 below as full and final remuneration.

7.2 INVOICING

a) On a date to be mutually agreed upon by both parties and according to schedules, CONTRACTOR shall submit to EMPLOYER detailed invoices in respect of the WORKS performed for each month. The invoices shall be submitted in one (1) original, clearly stamped 'ORIGINAL' and three (3) copies. The invoices shall;
- Bear reference to this Contract.
- Be supported by all necessary documentation to enable EMPLOYER to review and accept them.
- Clearly state the reason for which payments are required.

7.3 <u>PAYMENT</u>

a.   Payment, subject to the retention provisions under this Contract, shall be payable to CONTRACTOR in monthly instalments based on progress of WORKS. EMPLOYER shall have the sole authority to judge the progress of WORKS.

b.   Upon receipt of each invoice, EMPLOYER shall review it and if deemed to be in accordance with the Contract, EMPLOYER shall approve said invoice and payment shall be made to CONTRACTOR within the time stipulated in the "Appendix to Conditions".

c.   Should the invoice (the 'original invoice') be objected to wholly or in part by EMPLOYER, EMPLOYER shall within fifteen (15) days from receipt thereof return the invoice to CONTRACTOR for revision, specifying the item or items to which EMPLOYER objects and the reasons for such objection.

The amount claimed shall be for the value, proportionate to the amount of the contract, of work performed and products delivered to the SITE as of the last day of payment period.

Any payment made by EMPLOYER shall not be construed as a waiver of rights of EMPLOYER to object to any invoice so paid. EMPLOYER shall have the right to refuse any invoice not delivered by CONTRACTOR within six (6) months from the realization of relevant WORKS or engagement of relevant reimbursable costs, unless such invoice shall be a 'revised invoice', in which case EMPLOYER shall have the right to refuse receipt thereof if it is submitted more than six (6) months after the original invoice or prior revised invoice shall be objected to.

The payment procedure referred to in this sub-article shall apply mutatis mutandis to the payment of such amounts as they become due to CONTRACTOR because of variations or of other terms of this Contract.

Without waiver or limitation of any of its rights under the Contract or at law, EMPLOYER shall be entitled to deduct from any monies due to

CONTRACTOR under the Contract any amounts of any debt due from CONTRACTOR to EMPLOYER.

    d.   <u>Retention</u>

        i.   All payments to CONTRACTOR shall be subject to the withholding of a retention amounting to the percentage stipulated in the "Appendix to Conditions".

        ii.   Upon Provisional Acceptance of the WORKS, as provided for under Article 16, hereof, fifty percent (50%) of the retained amounts shall be released to CONTRACTOR. The remaining fifty percent (50%), shall be withheld by EMPLOYER until such date when CONTRACTOR has fully met his warranty and other obligations as contained in Articles 8 and 16 and provided that EMPLOYER shall have furnished CONTRACTOR with a FINAL ACCEPTANCE CERTIFICATE.

    e.   No payment shall be made by EMPLOYER until receipt of the performance bank guarantee required under article (9) and insurance policies as per article (10).

    f.   All invoices shall be presented and shall be payable in the currency stated in this Agreement.

    g.   EMPLOYER shall make payment to CONTRACTOR by direct transfer to the bank nominated by CONTRACTOR. CONTRACTOR shall give his bank's name and account number on or with each Invoice.

    h.   EMPLOYER shall give the CONTRACTOR notice in writing of any material change in the EMPLOYER's financial arrangements to fulfil the EMPLOYER's obligations under the contract during the performance of the contract.

8. **WARRANTIES**

8.1 CONSTRUCTION WARRANTY

a) CONTRACTOR warrants that the WORKS hereunder shall be free from defects, shall conform and perform as to comply with specifications and other requirements contained herein or other specifications mutually agreed upon.

b) Should CONTRACTOR before the issue of the PROVISIONAL ACCEPTANCE CERTIFICATE fail to carry out any up-keep or maintenance work deemed necessary by EMPLOYER. EMPLOYER shall have the right, after giving notice in writing to CONTRACTOR and if CONTRACTOR does not commence the said work within ten (10) days thereafter, to carry out or cause to be carried out such up-keep or maintenance work in such a manner as EMPLOYER deems appropriate then the costs, charges, expenses, and overheads in relation thereto as certified by EMPLOYER, shall be paid by CONTRACTOR.

c) For the period stated in the "Appendix to Conditions" after the date of issuance of the PROVISIONAL ACCEPTANCE CERTIFICATE. The CONTRACTOR shall, after written notice from EMPLOYER, repair or replace, at his own cost and expense, such materials, equipment or workmanship supplied or performed by him or his sub-contractors, which are not or shall not be in accordance with the specifications or otherwise defective. If CONTRACTOR fails to replace or repair such defective materials, equipment or workmanship noted above expeditiously, EMPLOYER should be entitled to arrange such replacements or repairs and to recover the cost from CONTRACTOR.

d) CONTRACTOR shall in each case likewise guarantee all materials, equipment or workmanship repaired or replaced pursuant to this warranty for the period specified in the "Appendix to Conditions" from the date of its being put into satisfactory operation.

8.2 SUPPLY WARRANTY

CONTRACTOR guarantees good title to all materials and equipment supplied by him and the fitness of such materials and equipment for the use intended. CONTRACTOR guarantees that: all materials, equipment, tools, and supplies designed, specified, arranged, used or installed by him in the WORKS shall conform to the specifications contained in the AGREEMENT. Such materials, equipment, tools, and supplies used or installed in the WORKS shall be procured only from good, reputable and responsible suppliers and that if any of such items shall be found defective, CONTRACTOR shall rectify or replace such defective item at his own cost.

CONTRACTOR shall obtain from his vendors and suppliers for the benefit of EMPLOYER all possible warranties with respect to materials, equipment, tools, and supplies delivered or installed by him, which warranties shall be assigned to EMPLOYER or to such entity as shall be designated by EMPLOYER, if EMPLOYER so directs.

Such warranties shall remain in force until the period specified in the "Appendix to Conditions" after the date of PROVISIONAL ACCEPTANCE CERTIFICATE. The same applicable to the warranties for materials, equipment, tools, and supplies are supplied or installed to rectify or replace any defect subsequently discovered, until the period specified in the "Appendix to Conditions" after such rectification or replacement work shall be provisionally accepted by EMPLOYER. CONTRACTOR's failure to obtain such warranties from his vendors and suppliers shall not relieve CONTRACTOR of his obligations with respect to materials, equipment, tools, and supplies procured from such vendors and suppliers.

When failure to perform in accordance with specifications results from defects in goods furnished by CONTRACTOR's vendors, CONTRACTOR shall take all actions available to him to enforce such warranties obtained from his vendors. CONTRACTOR shall keep EMPLOYER informed of all actions, which he shall take, and CONTRACTOR shall have the right to obtain from EMPLOYER an assignment to him of all rights of enforcement of such warranties.

8.3 DECENNIAL STRUCTURES WARRANTY

CONTRACTOR shall remain liable for a period of ten (10) years (*this period varies from country to another country*) for the soundness of the structures, as well as for any defect or error arising out of the performance of the WORKS, notwithstanding the issue of the FINAL ACCEPTANCE CERTIFICATE and the release of the Performance Bank Guarantee. CONTRACTOR shall also be liable for latent defects, frauds or errors becoming apparent after the issue of the FINAL ACCEPTANCE CERTIFICATE.

8.4 DESIGN WARRANTY

a) CONTRACTOR warrants that the structural design and the detailed engineering design carried out by himself shall be in accordance with good engineering practice and skill as is customarily employed. Such design shall conform to the requirements stated in the Contract.

b) In the event of any deficiency in EMPLOYER's design, CONTRACTOR's liability shall extend to giving notification of the defective design to EMPLOYER in proper time.

8.5 The foregoing warranties shall not be interpreted as a limitation upon but are in addition to all other warranties and guarantees expressed in the AGREEMENT or implied by law, custom or usage of trade, which shall apply in all respects to the WORKS.

9. **PERFORMANCE BANK GUARANTEE**

Within fifteen (15) days from the coming into force of this AGREEMENT, CONTRACTOR shall provide EMPLOYER with an unconditional and irrevocable Bank Guarantee. The Bank Guarantee shall be in accordance with the wording of ANNEX '**G**', by a bank in *enter the name of Province* acceptable to EMPLOYER and payable to EMPLOYER on first demand and valid up to the issue of the FINAL ACCEPTANCE CERTIFICATE.

The Bank Guarantee shall be in an amount equivalent to the percentage stated in the "Appendix to Conditions". This amount shall increase proportionally if the initially estimated CONTRACT PRICE increased.

The Bank Guarantee, the cost of which shall be borne by CONTRACTOR, shall be to secure CONTRACTOR's obligations under this AGREEMENT, notwithstanding any variations, alterations or extensions of time given or agreed upon.

10. **INDEMNITIES AND INSURANCES**

10.1 CONTRACTOR shall keep EMPLOYER, its servants or agents indemnified against claims, actions or proceedings brought or instituted against EMPLOYER, its servants or agents by any of his employees or any other third party in connection with, relating to, or arising out of the performance of the WORKS under this Contract.

10.2 CONTRACTOR shall indemnify EMPLOYER against any liability for any accident, death or injury to EMPLOYER's servants or agents or against any loss of or damage to any property belonging to EMPLOYER, its servants or agents that shall arise out of the performance of the WORKS under this Contract and against all costs, claims, demands and damages involved therewith.

10.3 Without limitation to CONTRACTOR's obligations and responsibilities during the whole period of the AGREEMENT from commencement until the issue of the FINAL ACCEPTANCE CERTIFICATE, CONTRACTOR shall obtain and maintain in the joint names of EMPLOYER, CONTRACTOR, ENGINEER and SUB-CONTRACTORS a **Workmen's Compensation and Employer's Liability Insurance** (with a limit of liability as stated in the "Appendix to Conditions"; a **Motor Vehicle Third Party and Passenger Liability Insurance** which shall provide an unlimited indemnity for death of or injury to persons and the equivalent amount stated in the "Appendix to

Conditions", and "**Board Form**" or **Employer's Property Insurance, insurance for Employer plant, equipment and property whether owned, hired, or leased** to their total value against all loss of or damage from whatever cause arising and shall cause the insurers or underwriters thereof to waive rights of subrogation against EMPLOYER, its subsidiaries and all other companies in EMPLOYER's group.

10.4 CONTRACTOR shall, prior to the commencement of any SITE activity submit all insurance policies to EMPLOYER for examination and approval, together with the evidence that the policy premium has been paid to the insurers, and shall remain in force throughout the duration of the Contract.

10.5 All deductibles or liabilities in excess of the indemnities provided under the insurances arranged by CONTRACTOR/SUB-CONTRACTOR and/or EMPLOYER shall be for the account of and paid by CONTRACTOR and his sub-contractors.

10.6 Without limitation to CONTRACTOR's obligations and responsibilities under this Contract and during the whole period of the Contract, CONTRACTOR, wherever, applicable, shall effect at its own expense in the joint names of EMPLOYER, CONTRACTOR, ENGINEER and SUB-CONTRACTORS a **Transit Insurance** of all ocean shipments, air freight movements and land transportation, **General Third Party Risks Insurance** of the WORKS, maintenance, materials and EMPLOYER's equipment, if any, excluding items which CONTRACTOR shall be already required to ensure at the commencement of the WORKS until completion of the same. The coverage should be 110% of the C&F part of the necessary equipment and material CONTRACT PRICE. The insurance shall cover all risks from ex-factory to job-sites until the starting of erection, including storage periods.

10.7 EMPLOYER shall not accept any responsibility whatsoever for any loss of or damage to any property or personal effects belonging to CONTRACTOR's employees or to those of SUB-CONTRACTORS.

10.9 The EMPLOYER and the CONTRACTOR shall indemnify and hold harmless the other from and against all claims, demands, losses, costs, damages, actions, suits, or proceedings arising out of their obligations in working with toxic and hazardous substances.

10.10 EMPLOYER shall indemnify and hold harmless from and against all claims, demands, losses, costs, damages, actions, suits or proceedings arising out of the CONTRACTOR's performance of the Agreement, which are attributable to a lack of or defect in title or an alleged lack of or defect in the Site of Works.

10.11 CONTRACTOR and/or SUB-CONTRACTORS shall notify insurers and EMPLOYER within fifteen (15) days of any occurrence likely to give rise to a claim under the insurance policies and shall handle all claims negotiations and submit relevant supporting documents to the insurers directly in co-ordination with EMPLOYER for final settlement to be effected to EMPLOYER's account. Subsequently CONTRACTOR and/or SUB-CONTRACTORS shall be reimbursed by EMPLOYER for the claim amount due, as the case shall be.

11. **TAXES AND DUTIES**

11.1 CONTRACTOR shall be liable for all taxes, imposts, duties, withholding taxes, charges or other assessments of whatsoever nature, whether levied by the Federal, Province Government in related to the WORKS site location.

11.2 All payments relating to sponsorship, which shall enable CONTRACTOR to work in the Province, Country, as well as all personal income tax or any corporate taxes or registration charges levied by the Federal or Provincial Government, shall be borne by CONTRACTOR.

11.3 All port dues, landing, pilotage, lighter age and other charges relating to the importation of materials and equipment shall be borne by CONTRACTOR.

11.4 The contract price shall include all taxes and custom duties in effect at the time of the bid closing date except for the value added taxes payable by the Employer to the Contractor as stated in the contract price paragraph of the Agreement.

11.5 Any increase or decrease in costs to the Contractor due to changes in such included taxes and duties after the time of the bid closing shall increase or decrease the contract price accordingly.

12. **VARIATIONS**

12.1 If a variation to the WORKS (hereinafter referred to as a "Variation") shall be required, during the currency of the Contract and until issue of the PROVISIONAL ACCEPTANCE CERTIFICATE, EMPLOYER shall initiate such Variation by forwarding to CONTRACTOR a statement describing the omissions in work or additional works to be performed.

CONTRACTOR shall make an estimate of the consequences of such Variation as to:

a) Time gained or reduced in respect of the time Schedule;
b) Expenses or savings anticipated;
c) Cost incurred by CONTRACTOR for performance of the additional work.

12.2 If EMPLOYER decides the Variation shall be carried out, they shall give CONTRACTOR its written acceptance thereof.

12.3 No such variation shall in any way vitiate or invalidate the Contract but the value, if any, of all such variations shall be taken into account in ascertaining the amount of the CONTRACT PRICE. The Schedule shall be adjusted to the extent necessary because of such variations.

12.4 No variation shall be paid where it shall be within the Scope of Work or shall be due to CONTRACTORS act or omission in complying with this AGREEMENT.

12.5 CONTRACTOR shall submit in writing full details of any claim or confirmation of any other instruction or development affecting the WORKS and for which he deems a Variation is required within reasonable time of the start of any additional expense to which CONTRACTOR shall consider himself entitled from EMPLOYER. After the lapse of the reasonable time, EMPLOYER shall consider no such claim. CONTRACTOR shall not postpone or delay the performance of the works for which he intends to claim, because it is subject to acceptance by EMPLOYER and/or finalisation of payment amount and/or time extension to the Schedule.

13. **SUSPENSION**

13.1 EMPLOYER shall have the right to suspend partly or as a whole at any time the performance of the WORKS. In such event, provided that such suspension shall not be otherwise provided for in the AGREEMENT or necessary by reason of default on CONTRACTOR's part, the extra reasonable cost incurred by CONTRACTOR under this Article shall be borne and paid by EMPLOYER, provided that CONTRACTOR shall not be entitled to recover any such extra cost unless he gives written notice of his intention to claim to EMPLOYER within twenty-eight (28) days of EMPLOYER's order. EMPLOYER shall settle and determine such extra payment and/or extension of time to be made to CONTRACTOR in respect of such claim as shall by mutual agreement be fair and reasonable.

13.2 Notwithstanding any dispute arising between CONTRACTOR and EMPLOYER during the achievement of the WORKS, CONTRACTOR shall bind himself not to suspend or delay partly or as a whole for any reason the performance of the WORKS.

13.3 CONTRACTOR can suspend or reduce the rate of the WORKS by giving within twenty one (21) days' notice to EMPLOYER when EMPLOYER fails in payment, to comply with a binding agreement or determination related to the WORKS, to comply with a binding dispute resolution taken by dispute board.

14. __TERMINATION__

14.1 EMPLOYER shall have the right to terminate this Contract by means of issuing a thirty (30) days' notice to CONTRACTOR, and without the need for any notice or resort to the courts, in, but not limited to any of the following cases:

i)   If CONTRACTOR delays the commencement of WORKS or shows any delay in the progress of WORKS in a manner, which, in the opinion of EMPLOYER, would not enable CONTRACTOR to complete WORKS within the period, prescribed.

ii) If CONTRACTOR stops or suspends the WORKS totally or any part thereof for a period of fifteen (15) successive days without appropriate reasons acceptable to EMPLOYER.

iii) If CONTRACTOR withdraws from or abandons the WORKS.

iv) If CONTRACTOR violates any of the terms and conditions of AGREEMENT or fails to fulfil any of his obligations under AGREEMENT and does not rectify the same within fifteen (15) days from the date of being notified of the same by EMPLOYER.

v)   If CONTRACTOR tries to deceive or defraud in his dealings with EMPLOYER.

vi) If CONTRACTOR offers, or tries implicitly or explicitly, to bribe any EMPLOYER's officer concerned with these works or EMPLOYER or any of his assistants or if he offers, to such persons, any donations, gifts, rewards to seduce such person or persons to do or to abstain from doing any act prejudicial to the interests of EMPLOYER.

vii) If CONTRACTOR becomes bankrupt or insolvent or commits any act that may cause him to become bankrupt or insolvent.

viii) In the event of liquidation of CONTRACTOR, as a firm.

ix) If CONTRACTOR refuses or omits to apply the instructions issued to him by EMPLOYER without reasonable justification, which should be duly submitted in writing, at the time, to EMPLOYER within twenty eight (28) days after receiving a written notice from EMPLOYER.

x) If CONTRACTOR assigns the AGREEMENT or any part thereof without the consent of EMPLOYER for the same.

14.2 EMPLOYER shall also have the right at its absolute discretion to terminate this AGREEMENT for any other reason. In such event of termination, EMPLOYER shall pay to CONTRACTOR for the work already performed up to termination plus reasonable costs incurred because of such termination.

14.3 On the termination of the WORKS, the following results will follow:

i) EMPLOYER shall make an inventory, within fifteen (15) days from the date of the notice of termination of the WORKS, of all the works completed together with all constructional plants, instruments, equipment and materials supplied to the site by CONTRACTOR. CONTRACTOR shall be informed by written notice, of the date of the inventory.

A minute of the inventory shall be made in the presence of both parties and the representatives of both parties. If CONTRACTOR or his engineer does not participate or refuses to sign the minute of the inventory, the same shall be noted therein and CONTRACTOR informed by written notice. If CONTRACTOR does not inform EMPLOYER, in writing, of his comments thereon, within seven (7) days of the receipt of such notice, such a failure shall be considered as agreement of CONTRACTOR in respect of the correctness of the inventory and the decision of EMPLOYER in regard to any objections or comments made by CONTRACTOR in this connection shall be final.

ii) Delay penalty shall be calculated in accordance with the AGREEMENT and up to the date on which notice of termination of the WORKS is served on CONTRACTOR.

iii) Any retentions from or amounts due to CONTRACTOR may be withheld until the final settlement of CONTRACTOR's accounts.

iv) Settlement of CONTRACTOR's account shall be made, and the dues to him, after the deduction of all rights and amounts resulting from the termination of the WORKS, shall be paid to CONTRACTOR.

v) In the case of sub-article 14.1 stated earlier, EMPLOYER shall be entitled to payment by the CONTRACTOR of:

a. The additional cost of execution of the Works‹ and all other costs reasonably incurred by the EMPLOYER including the costs of cleaning and reinstating the site.

b. Any losses and damages suffered by the EMPLOYER in completing the Works.

c. Delay Damages, if the Works or a section have not been taken over and if the date of termination occur after the date of corresponding to the time for completion of the Works or section (as the case may be). Such Delay Damages shall be paid for every day that has elapsed between these two dates.

d. EMPLOYER may withdraw and negotiate the Performance Bank Guarantee and deposit the same in favour of EMPLOYER until the final settlement of the account of CONTRACTOR.

14.4 The CONTRACTOR is entitled to give a notice to EMPLOYER of the CONTRACTOR's intention to terminate the contract if EMPLOYER fails to pay and does not inform CONTRACTOR within forty two (42) days after giving a notice to suspend the WORKS/or after any issued payment certificate. Moreover if EMPLOYER fails to pay CONTRACTOR within fifty six (56) days after receiving a statement and support document to issue relevant payment certificate.

15. **CLAIMS AND LIENS**

15.1 EMPLOYER shall have a first and paramount lien on all materials and equipment forming part of the WORKS. CONTRACTOR undertakes not to create or do any act, deed or thing which shall result in the creation of any other lien or charge on any materials or equipment forming or intended to form part of the WORKS.

15.2 Subject to any lien legislation applicable to the site of the WORKS, as of the fifth calendar day before the expiry of the lien period provided by the lien legislation applicable at the Site of the WORKS, the CONTRACTOR waives and releases the EMPLOYER from all claims which the CONTRACTOR has or reasonably ought to have knowledge of that could be advanced by the CONTRACTOR against the EMPLOYER arising from the CONTRACTOR's involvement in the WORKS, including, without limitation, those arising from negligence or breach of contract in respect to which the cause of action is based upon acts or omissions which occurred prior to or on the date of Professional Acceptance Certificate of the WORKS, except as follows;

a. Claims arising prior to or on the date of Professional Acceptance Certificate of the WORKS for which notice in writing of claim has been received by the EMPLOYER from the CONTRACTOR no later than the sixth calendar day before the expiry of the lien period provided by the lien legislation applicable to the Site of the WORKS.

b. Indemnification for claims advanced against the CONTRACTOR by third parties for which a right of indemnification may be asserted by the CONTRACTOR against the EMPLOYER pursuant to the provisions of this contract.

c. Claims for which the CONTRACTOR pursuant of Indemnification provisions of this contract could assert a right of indemnity.

d. Claims resulting from acts or omissions, which occur after the date of Professional Acceptance Certificate of the WORKS.

15.3 Subject to any lien legislation applicable to the site of the WORKS, as of the fifth calendar day before the expiry of the lien period provided by the lien legislation applicable at the site of the WORKS, the EMPLOYER waives and releases the CONTRACTOR from all claims which the EMPLOYER has or reasonably ought to have knowledge of that could be advanced by the EMPLOYER against the CONTRACTOR arising from the EMPLOYER's involvement in the WORKS, including, without limitation, those arising from negligence or breach of contract in respect to which the cause of action is based upon acts or omissions which occurred prior to or on the date of Professional Acceptance Certificate of the WORKS, except as follows;

a. Claims arising prior to or on the date of Professional Acceptance Certificate of the WORKS for which notice in writing of claim has been received by the CONTRACTOR from the EMPLOYER no later than the sixth calendar day before the expiry of the lien period provided by the lien legislation applicable to the Site of the WORKS.

b. Indemnification for claims advanced against the EMPLOYER by third parties for which a right of indemnification may be asserted by the EMPLOYER against the CONTRACTOR pursuant to the provisions of this contract.

c. Claims for which the EMPLOYER pursuant of Indemnification provisions of this contract could assert a right of indemnity.

d. Claims resulting from acts or omissions, which occur after the date of Professional Acceptance Certificate of the WORKS.

15.4 If at any time EMPLOYER shall receive notice or information of the recording of any such lien, or any evidence of any such lien or claim which, if valid, shall constitute a legal charge on the property of EMPLOYER and/or the materials or equipment and/or the WORKS or any part thereof or on any of CONTRACTOR's equipment not forming part of the materials or equipment or the WORKS, it shall forthwith communicate the receipt of such notice, information or evidence to CONTRACTOR.

15.5 If CONTRACTOR shall fail to pay or otherwise discharge such lien, or satisfy such claim, within a period of thirty (30) days after written notice from EMPLOYER pursuant to sub-article 15.3 above, EMPLOYER shall have the right to deduct and retain from monies due or to become due to CONTRACTOR, until such lien or claim shall be paid, discharged or released, a sum necessary to discharge such lien or claim.

16. **ACCEPTANCE, DEFICIENT WORK & REJECTION**

16.1 ACCEPTANCE

a. The WORKS shall be deemed to be provisionally accepted on the date stated on the PROVISIONAL ACCEPTANCE CERTIFICATE which shall be issued at the request of CONTRACTOR and when WORKS are performed to the satisfaction of EMPLOYER and in compliance with the terms of this Contract.

b. CONTRACTOR shall be entitled to request final acceptance, and an examination of WORKS. The operating conditions of the facilities shall be immediately arranged at the end of the period stated in the "Appendix to Conditions", which should be calculated from the date of the provisional acceptance of WORKS, and provided CONTRACTOR has entirely fulfilled his obligations under this Contract, including any work ordered pursuant to sub-article 16.2. EMPLOYER shall then issue the FINAL ACCEPTANCE CERTIFICATE, provided such examination was satisfactory to EMPLOYER and subject to the signing of the Release Letter by CONTRACTOR as per the format given in ANNEX 'H'.

c. The Warranty Period shall be intended particularly to ensure the proper performance of the WORKS during the specified period and the clearance therefrom of any defective material or deficient workmanship incorporated within the WORKS during the AGREEMENT period.

16.2 DEFICIENT WORKS AND REJECTION

a. If at any time before issue of the FINAL ACCEPTANCE CERTIFICATE there becomes apparent any failure of the WORKS, or part thereof to conform to the warranties, or any other defect, or deficiency in the WORKS for which CONTRACTOR shall be responsible, CONTRACTOR shall upon receipt of written notice from EMPLOYER at his own expense promptly remedy the same by, at EMPLOYER's option, repair or replacement.

b. If CONTRACTOR shall fail to promptly effect the required remedy then EMPLOYER shall be entitled to reject the part of the WORKS affected and to replace the same at CONTRACTOR's expense.

c. If EMPLOYER does not exercise its rights under the immediately preceding paragraph (b) within a reasonable time, CONTRACTOR shall not be relieved from liability in respect of the relevant non-conformity or other defect or deficiency but his full and complete responsibility shall be limited to the repayment of all monies paid by EMPLOYER to him in respect of the part of the WORKS affected thereby.

d. CONTRACTOR shall, if required by EMPLOYER, search for the cause of any malfunction, defect or deficiency in the WORKS and, if the same shall be found to be within the scope of CONTRACTOR's remedial responsibility as previously mentioned, the cost of the work carried out by CONTRACTOR in searching shall be borne by CONTRACTOR.

e. CONTRACTOR's failure to perform any of his obligations under this sub-article shall (without prejudice to any other rights which EMPLOYER shall have in the matter) result in EMPLOYER making demand under the Performance Bank Guarantee and/or any monies in their possession.

17. **CONFIDENTIALITY**

17.1 CONTRACTOR shall not, without the prior written consent of EMPLOYER, disclose, or make available to any person, other than EMPLOYER, or use, directly or indirectly, except for the performance and implementation of this Contract, any information acquired from EMPLOYER, its subsidiaries or affiliates in connection with the performance of this Contract.

17.2 CONTRACTOR shall take all steps, which shall be necessary or appropriate in order that his employees, agents and representatives adhere to the provisions of this article.

17.3 The obligations contained in this article shall continue, notwithstanding the issue of the FINAL ACCEPTANCE CERTIFICATE or the termination of the Contract.

17.4 Appropriate clauses to carry out the purpose and intent hereof shall be included in all sub-Contracts.

18. **ASSIGNMENT**

18.1 Neither party to the Contract shall assign the Contract or a portion thereof without the written consent of the other, which consent shall not be unreasonably withheld.

19. **SUB-CONTRACTING**

19.1 CONTRACTOR shall not sub-contract any part of the WORKS under this Contract without the prior written consent of EMPLOYER. Such consent shall not relieve CONTRACTOR of any of his obligations hereunder or create any contractual relations between EMPLOYER and his sub-contractors.

19.2 CONTRACTOR shall be fully responsible for any part of the WORKS performed by his sub-contractors and for their acts and omissions and those persons either directly or indirectly employed by them to the same extent, as he shall be for the acts and omissions of persons directly employed by CONTRACTOR.

19.3 CONTRACTOR is obliged not to sub contract whole the WORKS and should not exceed the percentage of the sub-contracted works, which agreed upon in the Contract.

20. **EXCEPTIONAL EVENTS**

20.1 If either party shall be temporarily rendered unable, wholly or in part, by Exceptional Event to comply with its obligations under this Contract, the effected party shall give a notice to other party of such an Exceptional Event, and shall specify the obligations, the performance of which is or will be prevented.

This notice shall be given within fourteen (14) days after the affected party become aware, or should have become aware, of the Exceptional Event, and the affected party shall then be excused performance of prevented obligations from the date such performance is prevented by the Exceptional Event. If the other party receives this notice after these 14 days, the affected party shall be excused performance of the prevented obligations only from the date on which the other party receives this notice. Thereafter, the affected party shall be excused performance of the prevented obligations for so long as such Exceptional Event prevents the affected party from performing them.

Other than performance of the prevented obligations, the affected party shall not be excused performance of all other obligations under the contract.

20.2 The obligations of either party to make payments due to other party under the contract shall not be excused by an Exceptional Event.

20.3 Neither party shall be liable for delays caused by Exceptional Event provided notice thereof shall be given as required above.

20.4 The term "Exceptional Event" as employed herein shall mean strikes (excluding strikes occurring among the employees of CONTRACTOR or his sub-contractors) or other industrial disturbances of general nature, acts of the public enemy, wars, blockades, insurrections, riots, epidemics, landslides, earthquakes, lightning, civil disturbances, explosions and any other cause similar to the kind herein enumerated or equivalent forces, not within the control of either party and which by exercise of due diligence neither party shall be able to overcome. In the event of any dispute, the party claiming to be affected by Exceptional Event shall bear the burden of proving that it has been so affected.

21. **ARBITRATION**

Any dispute, claim or difference arising out of or related to this Contract or breach thereof shall first be referred to the parties for an amicable settlement and shall, in the event such referral fails, be finally settled by arbitration in… *enter the name of the Chamber and laws*. The arbitration decision shall be final and binding on both parties and judgement upon the award of the arbitrators shall be entered in …*enter Province* court having jurisdiction thereof. The arbitration award shall be in lieu of any other remedy.

22. **APPLICABLE LAW**

22.1 The laws of… *enter name of Province/Country in related to the Works site location* shall apply to the construction, validity and performance of the Contract by CONTRACTOR. Such laws include without limitation any ordinance, rule, decree, regulation or order of any Governmental Authority or Agency of (State, National, Municipal, Local or other).

22.2 CONTRACTOR shall hold harmless, defend and indemnify EMPLOYER from and against any liability or penalty, which may be imposed by… *enter Federal or any Provincial or Territorial Governmental Authorities* on EMPLOYER by reason of any alleged violation or violation of the laws of *enter name of the Province of the Place of Works* arising out of his acts or omissions or of those of his employees while performing the WORKS.

22.3 CONTRACTOR shall give the required notices and comply with the laws, ordinances, rules, regulations, which are or become in force during the performance of the WORKS and which relate to the WORKS, to the preservation of the public health, and to construction safety.

23. **CONTRACT INTERPRETATION**

In the event of conflict between these General Conditions of the Contract, and any of their Annexes, Sections **B**" Technical specifications, Section **C**" Bill of Quantities /Pricing Schedules" and Section **D**" Drawings and Attachments" or any document incorporated by reference in the Contract, these Conditions of shall prevail. In the event of conflict between the Annexes and Sections **B**, **C**, and **D** in one part and documents incorporated in the other part, the document bearing the latest date shall prevail.

24. **ENTIRE CONTRACT**

This Contract embodies the entire agreement between CONTRACTOR and EMPLOYER with respect to the WORKS. The parties shall not be bound by or be liable for any statement, representation, promise, inducement or understanding of any kind or nature not set forth herein. No changes, amendments or modifications of the terms or conditions of this Contract shall be valid unless executed in writing and sign by both parties.

25. **INDEPENDENT CONTRACTOR**

CONTRACTOR shall act as an independent contractor in performing the WORKS, maintaining complete control over his employees and all of his sub-contractors and shall in no case represent EMPLOYER or act in its name without its prior written approval.

26. **WAIVER**

None of the terms or conditions of the Contract shall be considered waived by EMPLOYER or CONTRACTOR unless such waiver shall be given in writing to the other party. No such waiver shall be a waiver of any past or future default, breach or modifications of any of the terms or conditions of the Contract unless expressly stipulated in such waiver.

27. **PROTECTION OF PERSONS AND PROPERTY**

27.1 Protection of Work and Property

   a.   CONTRACTOR shall protect the Works and the EMPLOYER's property and property adjacent to the site of the WORKS from damage which may arise as the result of the CONTRACTOR's operations under the Contract, and shall be responsible for such damage except which occurs as the result of:
   1.   Errors in the Contract Documents.
   2.   Acts or omissions by the EMPLOYER, ENGINEER, other contractors.

   b.   Should the CONTRACTOR in the performance of the Contract damage the WORKS, the EMPLOYER's property or property adjacent to the site of the WORKS, the CONTRACTOR shall be responsible for repair or replace such damage at the CONTRACTOR's expense.

12.2 Toxic and Hazardous Substances [17]

   a.   For the purpose of applicable legislation related to toxic and hazardous substances, the EMPLOYER shall be deemed to have control and management of the site of the WORKS with respect to the exist conditions.
   b.   Prior to CONTRACTOR commencement of the Works, the EMPLOYER shall:
   1.   Take all reasonable steps to determine whether any toxic or hazardous substances are present at the site of the WORKS.
   2.   Provide the ENGINEER, and CONTRACTOR with written list of any such substances that are known on exist and their locations.

28. **ENGINEER'S DUTIES AND AUTHORITY**

28.1 The ENGINEER shall exercise the authority specified in or necessarily to be implied from the Contract on behalf of EMPLOYER, provided, however, that if the ENGINEER is required, under the terms of his appointment by EMPLOYER, to obtain the specific approval of EMPLOYER before exercising any such authority. Particulars of such requirements shall be as follows, provided further that any requisite approval shall be deemed to have been given by EMPLOYER for any such authority exercised by the ENGINEER:

i) Consenting to the Subletting of any part of the WORKS under article 19 "Sub-Contracting".

ii) Issuing a Variation Order or certifying additional costs, which have been determined, according to article 12: "Variations".

iii) Determining an Extension of Time for Completion and applying the Delay Penalty under article 3 "Duration".

iv) Notifying CONTRACTOR on suspension of WORKS.

28.2 Notwithstanding the obligation, as set out in sub-article 28.1 above, to obtain approval, if, in the opinion of the ENGINEER, an emergency occurs affecting the safety of life or of the WORKS or of adjoining property, he may, without relieving CONTRACTOR of any of his duties and responsibilities under the Contract, instruct CONTRACTOR to execute all such work or to do all such things as may, in the opinion of the ENGINEER, be necessary to abate or reduce the risk. CONTRACTOR shall forthwith comply, despite the absence of approval of EMPLOYER, with any such instruction of the ENGINEER. The ENGINEER shall determine an addition to the CONTRACT PRICE, in respect of such instruction, in accordance with article 12" Variations" and shall notify CONTRACTOR accordingly, with a copy to EMPLOYER.

28.3 Instructions given by the ENGINEER shall be in writing, if for any reason the ENGINEER considers it necessary to give any such instruction orally, CONTRACTOR shall comply with such instruction. Confirmation in writing of such oral instruction given by the ENGINEER, whether before or after the carrying out of the instruction, shall be deemed an instruction within the meaning of this sub-article. Provided further that if CONTRACTOR, within seven (7) days, confirms in writing to the ENGINEER any oral instruction of the ENGINEER and the ENGINEER does not contradict such confirmation in writing within seven (7) days, it shall be deemed an instruction of the ENGINEER.

29. **FOSSILS AND ANTIQUITIES**

29.1. All fossils, coins, monuments, articles of value or antiquity and structures or things of geological or archaeological value discovered on SITE shall as between the two parties, be deemed the absolute property of EMPLOYER.

29.2. CONTRACTOR shall take all reasonable precautions to prevent his workers or any other persons from removing or damaging any such articles or things and shall immediately on the discovery of such things and before their removal, inform EMPLOYER of such discovery and then carry out EMPLOYER's instructions for dealing with the disposal of the same at the expense. If because of such instructions, CONTRACTOR suffers delay and/or incurs costs then the disposal of the same shall be at the expense of EMPLOYER.

30. **COPYRIGHT**

All documents pertaining to this Contract shall be the exclusive property of EMPLOYER, it shall be entitled to use such documents in any works outside the scope of this Contract, and CONTRACTOR shall have no right to use such documents beyond the scope of this Contract.

31. **IN CASE OF DEMISE OF CONTRACTOR**

31.1 In the event of the death of CONTRACTOR, EMPLOYER may terminate the Contract and refund the performance bank guarantee to the heirs if there are no obligations towards EMPLOYER. EMPLOYER may allow the heirs to continue with carrying out the duties under the Contract if they appoint their representative who is to be approved by EMPLOYER.

31.2 If the Contract is one that has been concluded with more than one contractor and in the event of the death of one of them, EMPLOYER may terminate the CONTRACT and refund the performance guarantee after deducting all dues, or request the remaining contractors to continue with the performance of the CONTRACT.

31.3 In both the above cases the termination of the Contract shall be made by written letter with acknowledgement due, if it has been settled and resorted according to the applicable Federal, or Provincial law.

32. **NOTICES AND ADDRESSES**

Either party on the other shall serve any notice for the purpose of this Contract by sending the same by registered mail post or facsimile addressed to their respective addresses as hereinafter set out. Any and every such notice shall be effective upon first receipt and shall be addressed to the addresses stated in the "Appendix to Conditions", or to such other parties or addresses as either of the signed parties shall substitute by notice given as herein required.

33. **BANKRUPTCY**

If the CONTRACTOR should become bankrupt, or insolvent, or have a receiving order made against him, or compound with his creditors or, being a corporation, commence to be wound up, not being a member's voluntary winding up for the purpose of amalgamation or reconstruction, or carry out on its business under a receiver for the benefit of its creditors EMPLOYER shall be at liberty:

a.   To terminate the Contract forthwith by notice in writing to the CONTRACTOR, or the receiver or liquidator, or any person in whom the Contract may be vested.

In such event, EMPLOYER shall be entitled to seize and take possession of and have free use of all equipment, materials, tools, tackle or other items, which may be on the SITE, for use in connection with the execution of such Works and without being responsible to the CONTRACTOR for normal wear and tear of the same.

c. EMPLOYER shall also be entitled to retain and apply balance, which may otherwise then be due to CONTRACTOR under the CONTRACT, or such part thereof as may be necessary, to effect payment of the cost of execution of such previously mentioned work.

d. EMPLOYER may, at its sole discretion and against an acceptable bank guarantee of an agreed amount, elect not to terminate the CONTRACT, but to consider such receiver, liquidator or other person as CONTRACTOR's successor to carry out CONTRACTOR's obligations under the Contract.

34. **ADVANCE PAYMENT**

EMPLOYER will make an interest-free advance payment to the CONTRACTOR in respect of the WORKS for the amount stated in the "Appendix to Conditions" payable in the currency of the Contract Price, but in no event exceeding the amount stated in the "Appendix to Conditions". Payment of such advance amount will be due under separate invoice to be submitted to EMPLOYER after.

i) Submitting an original copy of the CONTRACT AGREEMENT signed by both parties.

ii) Provision by CONTRACTOR of the Performance Bank Guarantee in accordance with article (9) of the General Conditions; and

iii) Provision by CONTRACTOR of an unconditional bank guarantee issued in accordance with the wording of Annex 'G' by a bank in *enter the city/province* acceptable to EMPLOYER in amounts and currencies equal to the advance payment. Such bank guarantee shall be payable to EMPLOYER and remain effective until the advance payment has been repaid pursuant to the paragraph below, but the amount thereof shall be progressively reduced by the amount repaid by CONTRATOR as indicated in Interim Payment Invoices issued in accordance with this Article. The cost of the bank guarantee shall be borne by CONTRACTOR.

The advance payment shall be repaid through percentage deductions from the interim payments certified by EMPLOYER in accordance with this article. Deductions shall commence in the next Interim Payment Certificate and shall be made in equal percentages until such time as the advance payment has been repaid; provided always that the advance payment shall be completely repaid prior to the time when the total amount of the Contract Price has been certified for payment.

End of A1- General Conditions

A2. SPECIAL CONDITIONS

1. <u>INTERPRETATION OF SPECIAL CONDITIONS</u>

The following Special Conditions are specifying contractual requirements linked to the special circumstances of the overall project, and the contracted WORKS. They form part of the GENERAL Conditions of Contract, and in the event of any conflict between the General Conditions and the Special Conditions, the provisions of the Special Conditions complement and take precedence over those of the General Conditions.

2. <u>MATERIAL ACCEPTANCE</u>

CONTRACTOR shall not procure any material for use in WORKS unless he shall take prior approval from EMPLOYER. CONTRACTOR shall present specifications of materials to be used in WORKS for EMPLOYER's approval before placing the order.

3. <u>INSPECTION BY EMPLOYER</u>

EMPLOYER's representative shall inspect CONTRACTOR's works at each stage, and shall either accept or reject the same. CONTRACTOR shall rectify the rejected work, entirely at his own cost and to the entire satisfaction of EMPLOYER.

4. **FOOD AND ACCOMMODATION**

CONTRACTOR shall be responsible for food and accommodation of CONTRACTOR's SITE personnel assigned for the WORKS under this Contract.

5. **TEMPORARY WORKS**

CONTRACTOR shall carry out all temporary works necessary for the completion of WORKS and shall remove them and clear the area as soon as the WORKS are complete.

6. **RESTRICTED AREA** [*If applicable*]

CONTRACTOR shall fully recognise that the SITE shall be a restricted area and that all WORKS and movement within it shall be subjected to the regulations and instructions of the Federal, or any Provincial or Territorial Government Rules.

7. **HAZARDOUS AREA** [*If applicable*]

The work area shall be in and around the operating units, which shall be considered a hazardous area. CONTRACTOR shall fully familiarise himself with the safety rules/regulations and work permit procedures. If CONTRACTOR shall experience unavoidable interruption of work due to operational or safety reasons, such delays/interruptions shall not entitle CONTRACTOR to reimbursement of additional costs.

8. **SUPERINTENDENCE**

CONTRACTOR shall give or provide all necessary superintendence as necessary for the proper fulfilling of CONTRACTOR's obligations under this Contract.

9. **SCAFFOLDING**

If scaffolding shall be required for safe performance of the WORK, CONTRACTOR shall erect the same using his own standard steel scaffolding materials. The use of wooden scaffolding shall not be permitted. CONTRACTOR shall ensure that the scaffolding shall be erected in such a manner so as not to interfere with other activities in the area.

10. **TEST AREAS FOR INSPECTION**

In order to facilitate the determination of inspection procedures CONTRACTOR shall if so instructed by EMPLOYER prepare to predetermined standards test and sample areas. This work shall be deemed included in CONTRACTORS lump sum prices for the WORKS.

11. **CLEANING UP**

CONTRACTOR shall maintain a high standard of housekeeping around the working area and shall provide any covers, screens etc. necessary to protect adjoining areas not affected by the WORKS.

CONTRACTOR shall at all time, keep the working area including adjoining premises, in a neat, clean and safe condition. Upon completion of any portion of the WORKS, CONTRACTOR shall promptly remove all his equipment, construction plant, temporary works and surplus materials not to be used at or near the same location during later stages of WORKS.

12. **WORKING HOURS**

EMPLOYER normal working hours are (*enter the number as per the Province or* Territorial regulations) hours per week spread over five days. CONTRACTOR shall carry out the WORK daily during the working hours agreed upon and shall not perform any part of the WORKS nor allow any other person other than the watchman to stay at the SITE beyond such time or during the night or on rest days without a written authorisation from EMPLOYER. Such authorisation shall not cause CONTRACTOR to be entitled to claim any additional payments nor exempt him from any obligations under this Contract.

13. **TERMS OF PAYMENT**

Payments under this Agreement shall be effected in *enter the currency of the contract* for both the material, and for erection as stipulated in this Contract.

Reference should be made to the specific General Conditions for the underlying rules and regulations governing payments. All payments to CONTRACTOR shall be subject to withholding of a retention as specified in article 7.3 (d) of the General Conditions. The various items of the Contract Price shall become due and payable to CONTRACTOR in monthly instalments (monthly progress payments) in the following manner (before applying the retention): -

i. **For the Supply of Material Part:**

   1. CIF Material and Plants to be used in the WORKS

       a. Twenty percent (20%) upon CONTRACTOR's presentation of complete shipping documents pro-rata for each consignment.
       b. Forty percent (40%) upon presentation of CONTRACTOR's "Receiving Cum Damage Reports" pro-rata for each consignment‹ provided that the material be in conformity with specifications and conditions of Contract.
       c. Forty percent (40%) in monthly progress payment upon erection of plants at site and/or installation of material in place.

   2. Domestic Purchased Material and Plants be used in the WORKS.

       a. Sixty percent (60%) upon presentation of the CONTRACTOR's "Receiving-cum-Damage Reports" pro-rata for each consignment with delivery note from domestic supplier‹ provided that the material be in conformity with specifications and conditions of Contract.

b. Forty percent (40%) in monthly progress payment upon erection of plants at site and/or installation of material in place.

3. <u>CIF Spare Parts</u>

a. Twenty percent (20%) upon CONTRACTOR's presentation of complete shipping documents pro-rata for each consignment.

b. Sixty percent (60%) upon presentation of CONTRACTOR's "Receiving-cum-Damage Reports" pro-rata for each consignment‹ provided that the material is in conformity with specifications and conditions of AGREEMENT.

c. Twenty percent (20%) upon CONTRACTOR's complete delivery of the acceptable spares to EMPLOYER's stores against issuance of Stores Receipt Voucher (or Good receipt note-GRN).

4. <u>Domestic Purchased Spare Parts</u>

a. Eighty percent (80%) upon presentation of CONTRACTOR's "Receiving-cum-Damage Reports" pro-rata for each consignment with delivery note from the domestic supplier‹ provided that the spare parts be in conformity with specifications and conditions of Contract.

b. Twenty percent (20%) upon CONTRACTOR's complete delivery of the acceptable spares to EMPLOYER's stores against issuance of Stores Receipt Voucher.

ii. **For Erection, Construction, Installation and Other Expenses Part:**

a. One Hundred percent (100%) in monthly progress payments for works at site as approved by EMPLOYER.

iii. **Surplus Material:**

1. <u>Surplus CIF Material,</u> (provided not to exceed 15% of the Contract materials)

   a. Twenty percent (20%) upon CONTRACTOR's presentation of complete shipping documents pro-rata for each consignment.
   b. Forty percent (40%) upon presentation of CONTRACTOR's "Receiving Cum Damage Reports" pro-rata for each consignment‹ provided that the material is in conformity with specifications and conditions of Contract.
   c. Forty percent (40%) upon delivery of the materials to EMPLOYER's stores against issuance of Stores Receipt Voucher.

2. <u>Surplus Domestic purchased Material,</u> (provided not to exceed 15% of the Contract materials)

   a. Sixty percent (60%) upon presentation of CONTRACTOR's "Receiving-cum-Damage Reports" pro-rata for each consignment with delivery note from the domestic supplier‹ provided that the material is in conformity with specifications and conditions of Contract.
   b. Forty percent (40%) upon delivery of the materials to EMPLOYER's stores against issuance of Stores Receipt Voucher.

End of A2-Special Conditions

A3- APPENDIX TO CONDITIONS

- *This sub-section usually filled by EMPLOYER before issuance of the Tender Documents (RFP).*
- *EMPLOYER should insert relevant data for all the appropriate blank spaces prior to the issue of the Tendering Documents (RFP).*
- *Below a form and sample of an "appendix to Conditions", EMPLOYER can modify and add more conditions and details.*

The Appendix to Conditions is forming part of the Conditions of Contract (Section A). It incorporates Information that specifies and complements the provisions of the General Conditions. It also amends and/or supplements the provisions of the General Conditions. The provisions of the Appendix to Conditions take precedence over those of the General Conditions (Section A1).

GENERAL CONDITIONS OF AGREEMENT	ARTICLE No.	DETAILS *"To be defined and completed and floated with the Tender(RFP)"*
Definitions: SITE	1.	Summarise all locations where WORKS to be performed.
Definitions: ENGINEER	1.	Engineer's Name and Address, if applicable
AMOUNT OF DELAY PENALTY	3.2.a)	_____ Percent per week (or pro rata on a daily basis). *[Usually One (1%) per week for WORKS]*
LIMIT OF DELAY PENALTY	3.2.a)	_____ Percent of the final AGREEMENT PRICE. *[Usually Ten (10%) percent]*

INSPECTION OF THE SITE	6.4	Data made available by EMPLOYER under sub-article 6.4 is open for inspection at *[Insert address. If applicable, the SITE is open for inspection at any time.]*
PAYMENT PERIOD	7.3.b)	() days from the receipt correct invoice by EMPLOYER. *[Usually forty five (45) days]*
RETENTION MONEY	7.3.d.i)	() percent of the gross value of all certified payments. *[Usually ten (10%) percent]*
PERIOD OF CONSTRUCTION WARRANTY	8.1.c)	() months after the date of issue of the PROVISIONAL ACCEPTANCE CERTIFICATE.
REPLACED SUPPLY	8.1.d)	() months from the date of being put into satisfactory operation.
PERIOD OF SUPPLY WARRANTY	8.2	Until () months after the date of PROVISIONAL ACCEPTANCE CERTIFICATE.
PERIOD OF DEFECTED SUPPLY WARRANTY	8.2	Until () months after such rectification or replacement work shall be provisionally accepted by EMPLOYER
PERFORMANCE BANK GUARANTEE	9.	The Performance Bank Guarantee shall be in an amount equivalent to ten (10%) percent of the initially estimated Agreement Price in the form of an "unconditional irrevocable bank guarantee".
MINIMUM AMOUNT OF INDEMNITIES AND INSURANCES	10.3	The limit of liability shall be as follows: • Workmen's Compensation and Employer's Liability Insurance: The amount shall not be less than $..... Million per occurrence. • The Motor Vehicle Third Party and Passenger Liability Insurance: The amount shall be the equivalent of not less $..... Million For loss of or damage to property. CONTRACTOR shall confirm in writing that the vehicles covered under the policy are the only ones utilized for the Contract.

LIMIT OF VARIATIONS	12.	EMPLOYER reserves the right to amend the entire contents of the AGREEMENT by increasing, decreasing or omitting any work included in the AGREAMENT within the limit of twenty (20%) percent of the CONTRACT PRICE.
FINAL ACCEPTANCE	16.1 b	_____ (___) months from the date of issue of the Provisional Acceptance Certificate.
NOTICE AND ADRESSES	32.	**EMPLOYER's address is:** .... **CONTRACTOR's address is:** .... *[CONTRACTOR should insert the name and address of his firm]*
ADVANCE PAYMENT	34.	Ten (10%) percent of the initially estimated Contract Price provided that not to exceed $.... ...million.

End of A3- Appendix to Conditions

A4. ANNEXES

ANNEX A.   Scope of Work:

                1. Scope of Work

                2. Quality Control and Assurance

ANNEX B.   List of Drawings and Attachments

ANNEX C.   Free Issue Materials List

ANNEX D.   Facilities provided by *enter Employer name*

ANNEX E.   Co-ordination Procedure

ANNEX F.   Safety Regulations

ANNEX G.   Bank Guarantees:

                1. Form of Performance Bank Guarantee

                2. Form of Advance Payment Bank Guarantee

ANNEX H.   Acceptance Certificates and Release Letter:

                1. Provisional Acceptance Certificate

                2. Final Acceptance Certificate

                3. Release Letter.

ANNEX I *   Schedules:

                1. Key Dates

                2. Overall Schedule

                3. Contractor's Labour Histograms

                4. Contractor's Proposed Work Plan, Supplies and Methods

ANNEX J *   Key Personnel

ANNEX K. *   Subcontractors and Associates List

ANNEX L. *   Contractor's Proposed Temporary Facilities on Site

These Annexes to be completed by the CONTRACTOR.

ANNEX 'A'

1. SCOPE OF WORK

Insert the scope of the WORKS here

2. QUALITY CONTROL AND ASSURANCE

2.1 CONTRACTOR'S RESPONSIBILITIES

2.1.1 QUALITY CONTROL

CONTRACTOR shall be responsible for producing a Quality Control Procedure for implementation. The procedure shall contain inspection report forms and test report forms to record the quality of the materials and workmanship, in accordance with the requirements of the Contract. Where applicable such reports shall contain details of weather conditions, humidity, temperature and particulars of application.

The Procedures shall only be implemented with the approval of EMPLOYER.

CONTRACTOR shall appoint an Inspection Engineer to implement the Quality Control Procedure. CONTRACTOR's Inspection Engineer shall be responsible for preparing the weekly Quality Control Reports, two copies of which together with all corresponding test and inspection report forms shall be transmitted to EMPLOYER.

2.1.2 QUALITY ASSURANCE

CONTRACTOR shall be responsible for producing and implementing a Quality Assurance Plan to ensure that inspection and testing of the WORKS is carried out in accordance with the relevant provisions of the Contract. CONTRACTOR shall appoint suitably qualified and experienced personnel to implement the approved Quality Assurance Plan.

2.1.3 TESTING

Testing shall be in accordance with the requirements of the Contract. CONTRACTOR shall keep a full formal record. CONTRACTOR shall inform EMPLOYER at least twenty four (24) hours in advance of all tests requiring witnessing so that EMPLOYER can be present for the test. For specific tests, witness tests and hold points, CONTRACTOR should refer to the Inspection and Test Plans (ITPs) which form part of the Technical Specifications.

2.2 INSPECTION AND TESTING BY EMPLOYER

2.2.1 GENERAL

EMPLOYER shall have the right to inspect at all times any tools, instruments, materials, staging, or equipment used or to be used in the performance of the WORKS. CONTRACTOR shall make all parts of the WORK accessible for these inspections. For specific tests, witness tests and hold points, CONTRACTOR should refer to the Inspection and Test Plans (ITPs) which form part of the Technical Specifications.

2.2.2 REJECTED WORK AND EQUIPMENT

EMPLOYER shall have the right to condemn all tools, instruments, materials, staging, equipment, or work which does not conform to specifications.

CONTRACTOR shall rectify any defective work not conforming to specifications at no additional cost to EMPLOYER. Any condemned tools, instruments, materials, or equipment shall be replaced or rectified at no additional costs to EMPLOYER.

2.2.3 APPROVAL

CONTRACTOR shall notify EMPLOYER Twenty Four (24) hours before work or part of the work commences. Prior to final acceptance of part of or the complete work, an inspection shall be made. CONTRACTOR shall make an inspection report, which shall be signed by all parties.

2.3 <u>ACCEPTANCE OF COMPLETED WORK</u>

2.3.1 Daily and in a reasonable time before leaving the SITE, a full report on outstanding and/or incomplete and/or remedial work shall be submitted to EMPLOYER for final approval.

2.3.2 The Inspection Check List and Test Reports shall be used as back up for Completion Certificates for the WORKS. The Completion Certificate shall be signed and dated by a Representative of CONTRACTOR and EMPLOYER to accept the WORKS.

ANNEX 'B'

List of Drawing and Attachments

{LIST DOWN ALL DRAWINGS AND ATTACHMENTS}

ANNEX 'C'

FREE ISSUE MATERIALS LIST

[To be listed, if EMPLOYER shall issue any material for the WORKS included in this Contract]

ANNEX 'D'

FACILITIES PROVIDED BY EMPLOYER

1.0 EMPLOYER shall provide such facilities and services specified herein, to CONTRACTOR as per EMPLOYER's standards and procedures. A minimum period of one week shall be required for the provision of such services after receipt from CONTRACTOR of a written request for the same.

2.0 EMPLOYER shall provide Letters to Assist CONTRACTOR in securing necessary Licences, Work Permits, Security Passes, Documentation and egress of Personnel, Equipment and operations in *enter the name of Province/ Territory* in connection with this AGREEMENT. The provision of such Letters of Assistance shall not be construed so as to hold EMPLOYER liable for any delays in obtaining the said Licences, Work Permits, Security Passes, Documentation and egress of Personnel, Equipment and operation in *enter the name of Province/ Territory*, or for not obtaining the same for any reason whatsoever.

ANNEX 'E'

CO-ORDINATION PROCEDURE

This procedure outlines the various responsibilities of the Representatives nominated by EMPLOYER and CONTRACTOR for the above Contract. CONTRACTOR shall carry out proper execution of the WORKS under supervision of EMPLOYER's Representative for this project.

1. COMMUNICATION

The English language shall be used for all correspondence, reports, instruction, drawings, specifications, and more.

As far as possible, all written communication shall be at SITE level directly between EMPLOYER and CONTRACTOR. All efforts shall be made to keep the correspondence to the minimum. If, for expediency, telephonic conversation shall be used, both parties shall confirm this in writing within two (2) working days.

Notwithstanding the provisions of article 32 "Notices and Addresses" of the General Conditions, hand delivery shall be an approved means of exchange of letters.

CONTRACTOR shall prepare and issue the Minutes of all his meetings with EMPLOYER and shall be responsible for obtaining approval of these minutes prior to release within two (2) working days.

2. SITE INSTRUCTIONS

Instructions shall be confirmed in writing, using a numbered SITE Instruction signed by EMPLOYER. CONTRACTOR's representative shall be required to sign one copy of each instruction as confirmation of its receipt.

3. <u>REPORTS</u>

EMPLOYER shall require the reports mentioned below. They shall be handed over to EMPLOYER as required.

i.   Monthly Site Progress Reports (MSPR)

These reports shall include and cover detailed listing of work performed by CONTRACTOR during the past month as well as a summary of works completed to date, charts and photographs and detailed listing of work to be performed during the coming month. The MSPR shall be submitted to EMPLOYER in five (5) copies within one week after the end of the reporting period.

ii. Weekly Report (Construction Progress Report)

A detailed report shall be prepared showing percentage completion figures in both tabular and graphical formats. The completion figures shall show actual completion compared to scheduled, planned work force versus the actual on SITE and shall be broken down into individual disciplines.

A detailed narrative shall also accompany this report describing highlights and an analysis of the construction progress.

Any deviation from the agreed schedule shall be identified.

CONTRACTOR shall submit Two (2) copies of this report on (*enter the day and timing*)

iii. Daily Report

CONTRACTOR shall prepare a standard form for Daily Reports, which shall be approved by EMPLOYER. It shall become the Daily Field Log. The information required shall be as follows:

a.   A breakdown, by craft, of work force and major equipment used by CONTRACTOR and his sub-contractors on SITE.

    b.   Construction highlights.

    c.   Any other problems, which shall affect the progress of the WORKS.

This log shall be prepared and maintained daily at SITE and a copy shall be delivered to EMPLOYER's representative next morning.

4.   <u>PERFORMANCE AND PLANNING</u>

At the commencement of this Contract, CONTRACTOR shall detail his programme with actual dates shown on the bar charts.

Such activity on this bar chart shall indicate construction stages to meet requirement for target assessments.

Meeting(s) with EMPLOYER shall be held when CONTRACTOR shall report programme status at that time and planned construction activities for the coming week. The minutes of such meeting(s) shall be written by CONTRACTOR and approved by EMPLOYER.

All planning documents shall be updated weekly and submitted to EMPLOYER as part of the construction progress report.

5.   <u>PERMITS/PERMISSIONS</u> [*If applicable*]

5.1 Security passes

When there is a security authority appointed at the SITE, all work force shall take all necessary instructions and regulations seriously and getting passes in order to avoid external people to enter the SITE.

5.2 Site Work Permits

When undertaking work requiring a permit, CONTRACTOR shall assist and co-ordinate with EMPLOYER to comply with requirements for safety and operation until the permit shall be obtained, in strict compliance with EMPLOYER procedure, each morning, before commencing work in the designated area. Site work permits shall be in accordance with EMPLOYER's Safety/Security Regulations.

5.3 Any delay or expenses for securing necessary permission/permits/passes from the concerned authorities shall not entitle CONTRACTOR to any claim for extension of completion date or payment.

ANNEX 'F'

SAFETY REGULATIONS

EMPLOYER shall provide CONTRACTOR at SITE, wherever applicable, a copy of its Safety and Security Regulations in respect of WORKS on site. It shall be the responsibility of CONTRACTOR to ensure strict adherence to such Regulations.

ANNEX 'G'

BANK GUARANTEES

1. FORM OF PERFORMANCE BANK GUARANTEE

Below the wording of Performance Bank Guarantee, (*to be typed on original head letter of the Guarantor/Bank*)

Guarantee No; *enter the guarantee reference number*
The Guarantor: *enter the name and address of the bank, unless indicated on the letterhead.*
Contract Title / Contract No; *enter the name and number of the Contract between the Applicant and the Beneficiary on which the guarantee is based.*
The Beneficiary (the "**EMPLOYER**"); *enter the name and address of the Beneficiary.*

We have informed that ...*enter the name and address of the Contractor...* (the "**Applicant**") is your Contractor under such Contract, which require him/her to obtain a Performance Bank Guarantee.

At the request of the Applicant, we...*enter name and address of the Bank...* hereby irrevocably undertake to pay you, the Beneficiary/EMPLOYER, any sum or sums not exceeding in total ...*enter in figures and words the maximum amount payable and currency in which it is payable..*(the "Guaranteed Amount") upon receipt by us of your demand in writing and your written statement indicating in what respect the Applicant is in beach of its obligations under the Contract.

We agree that any changes, modifications, additions, or amendments which may be made to the Contract, or in the work to be performed thereunder, or in the payments to be made on account thereof, or any extensions of the time for performance or other forbearance on the part of either Beneficiary/EMPLOYER or Applicant /CONTRACTOR to the other or to any other guarantor of the obligations of either of them, shall not in any way release us from our continuing liability hereunder, and we

---

hereby expressly waive notice to us of any such changes, modifications, additions, amendments, extensions or forbearance.

We further agree that any payment made hereunder shall be made free and clear of and without deductions for or on account of any present or future taxes, levies, imposts, duties, charges, fees, deductions or withholdings of any nature whatsoever and by whomsoever imposed.

This Performance Bank Guarantee shall come into force on the date hereof *enter the date* and shall continue valid and enforceable until the issue of the Final Acceptance Certificate.

This Performance Bank Guarantee shall be governed by and interpreted under the laws of...*enter the Province or Territory laws.*

Signed By :
Name;
Date;

2. FORM OF ADVANCE PAYMENT BANK GUARANTEE

Below the wording of Advance Payment Bank Guarantee, (*to be typed on original head letter of the Guarantor/Bank*)

Guarantee No; *enter the guarantee reference number*

The Guarantor: *enter the name and address of the bank, unless indicated on the letterhead.*

Contract Title / Contract No; *enter the name and number of the Contract between the Applicant and the Beneficiary on which the guarantee is based.*

The Beneficiary (the "**EMPLOYER**"); *enter the name and address of the Beneficiary.*

We have informed that ...*enter the name and address of the Contractor...* (the "**Applicant**") is your Contractor under such Contract, wish to receive an advance payment, which the Contract requires him/her to obtain a guarantee.

At the request of the Applicant, we..*enter name and address of the Bank..* hereby irrevocably undertake to pay you, the Beneficiary/EMPLOYER, any sum or sums not exceeding in total ...*enter in figures and words the maximum amount payable and currency in which it is payable..*(the "Guaranteed Amount") upon receipt by us of your demand in writing and your written statement that;

    a. The Applicant has failed to repay the advance payment in accordance with the Conditions of Contract, and

    b. The amount of the advance payment which the Applicant has failed to repay

We agree that any changes, modifications, additions, or amendments which may be made to the Contract, or in the work to be performed thereunder, or in the payments to be made on account thereof, or any extensions of the time for performance or other forbearance on the part of either Beneficiary/ EMPLOYER or Applicant/ CONTRACTOR to the other or to any other guarantor of the obligations of either of them, shall

---

not in any way release us from our continuing liability hereunder, and we hereby expressly waive notice to us of any such changes, modifications, additions, amendments, extensions or forbearance.

This guarantee shall become effective upon receipt "of the first installment" of the advance payment by the Applicant. The guarantee amount shall be reduced by the amounts of the advance payment repaid to you, as evidence by monthly payment certificates issued under the conditions of the Contract by the Beneficiary/EMPLOYER.

This Bank Guarantee shall remain valid until it is called up or you inform us that it is canceled.

This Advance Payment Bank Guarantee shall be governed by and interpreted under the laws of.. *Enter the Province or Territory laws.*

Signed By :
Name;
Date;

ANNEX 'H'

ACCEPTANCE CERTIFICATES AND RELEASE LETTER

1. PROVISIONAL ACCEPTANCE CERTIFICATE (PAC)

Below sample of provisional acceptance certificate

CONTRACT Title /NO.: .... Date: ....

PART - I
DESCRIPTION OF WORKS

....

....

PART - II

The above WORKS have been completed in accordance with the provisions of the CONTRACT, except for those items enumerated in Appendix (x), and are now handed over to *enter the name of EMPLOYER*, subject to the Warranty conditions contained in the CONTRACT.

CONTRACTOR: ....

By: .... Date:

PART - III

The above WORKS have been provisionally accepted with effect from .... on behalf of *enter the name of EMPLOYER* in good order with the exceptions as described in Appendix (x), subject to the Warranty conditions contained in the CONTRACT, effective from *enter the date*

EMPLOYER: ....

By: .... Date: ....

Title: ....

APPENDIX 1

EXCEPTIONS TO COMPLETION,
Appendix (x) is an attachment incorporated with this PAC
List all items, which are exception to complete.

2. FINAL ACCEPTANCE CERTIFICATE (FAC)

Below sample of Final Acceptance Certificate.

CONTRACT Title/ NO....   Date: ....

PART - I

DESCRIPTION OF WORKS

....

....

FINAL PAYMENT DUE FROM EMPLOYER TO CONTRACTOR IS *enter in figures and words the amount and currency in which it is payable.*

PART - II

The above WORKS have been finally completed in accordance with the provisions of the CONTRACT and final payment is now due.

_____

For and on behalf of: (CONTRACTOR)

PART - III

The above WORKS have been finally accepted on behalf of EMPLOYER in apparent good order; with effect from ...enter the date................

For and on behalf of: EMPLOYER.

---

3. RELEASE LETTER

Below sample of the Release Letter. (*To be typed on original CONTRACTOR's head letter*)

Date: ....

CONTRACT TITLE/ No.: ...enter contact title and number

Entered into on;...*enter the Contract signature date*

Between

enter name of EMPLOYER
And
Enter name of CONTRACTOR..

For the provision of ....enter the Work and name of the project

KNOW ALL ATTENDEES BY THESE PRESENTS,

THAT CONTRACTOR, for and in consideration of the receipt of the sum of *enter in figures and words the amount and currency* by CONTRACTOR from EMPLOYER representing the final payment under the above CONTRACT dated the .... day of ...., and subsequent amendments between CONTRACTOR and EMPLOYER, hereby releases and forever discharges EMPLOYER, its successors-in-interest, assignees, and their property from all claims and demands whatsoever in any manner arising out of, or related to the said CONTRACT or labor performed or materials and equipment furnished by CONTRACTOR in connection with, or incidental to, the execution and completion of the WORKS.

In consideration of, and for the purpose of inducing EMPLOYER to issue the FINAL ACCEPTANCE CERTIFICATE and make the aforesaid final payment, CONTRACTOR hereby represents, warrants and agrees that;

---

1) All sums due or to become due and all debts, accounts damages, obligations, claims and demands of every nature and kind whatsoever in any manner arising out of, or related to, labor performed or materials and equipment furnished in connection with, or incidental to, the CONTRACT have been paid and satisfied.

2) There are no unsettled claims for injuries to, or death of, any persons or damage to, or destruction of, property in any manner arising out of, or related to, the CONTRACT.

3) CONTRACTOR shall indemnify and hold harmless EMPLOYER and its successors and assignees from and against any claims, demands, liens, judgements, attachments, and costs related hereto in any manner, arising out of, or related to, the CONTRACT.

4) CONTRACTOR acknowledges his continuing liability to EMPLOYER for executing, without further payment, all works of repair, amendment, reconstruction, rectification and making good defects, imperfections, shrinkage or other faults as shall have been or be required in writing by EMPLOYER during the Maintenance Period or within fourteen (14) days after its expiration, in connection with, or incidental to, the WORKS.

In witness whereof CONTRACTOR has caused this instrument to be executed by his duly authorised representative(s) this.............. day of ....

For and on behalf of CONTRACTOR:

....…..................

AUTHORISED SIGNATURE
BY: ....…......................…..........[Name]

TITLE: ...

In the capacity of: ....

In the presence of: ....

ANNEX 'I'

SCHEDULE

1. Key Dates (commencement, completion if not defined by EMPLOYER)

1.1 Date for commencement of Mobilisation

The date of Commencement of Mobilisation for temporary works, construction plant and facilities shall be deemed the Effective Date i.e Letter of Acceptance (Letter of Award) date.

1.2 Date for commencement of WORKS

The date of commencement of the WORKS shall be .... (.........) days from the Effective Date.

1.3 Date for completion of WORKS

The date for completion of the WORKS shall be .... (.........) days from the Effective Date.

1.4 Date for completion of Construction Warranty Period

The date for completion of warranty period shall be .... (...) days from the date of issue of Provisional Acceptance Certificate.

2. Overall Schedule (CONTRACTOR's Bar Chart, preferably with Critical Path)

{*List down the detailed bar chart with anticipated schedule, which was submitted by the CONTRACCTOR during tendering, it is covered all the activities and areas required to complete the Works. The schedule must show all dates of deliveries of all activities needed to complete the obligations of the CONTRACTOR and EMPLOYER approved that}.*

3.   CONTRACTOR's Labour Histograms

{List down the labour histograms anticipated for the duration of the Works that indicates; Site staff and Labour needed}

4.   CONTRACTOR/Tenderer's Proposed Work Plan, Supplies and Methods

{List down the CONTRACTOR's description of the arrangements, sequences and methods of construction of the Works which was approved by EMPLOYER supported with schedule of materials that shall be utilised for the execution of the Works incorporated with full technical specifications and manufacturer's instructions with the list of equipment, machineries and tools needed for completion of the works}.

ANNEX 'J'

KEY PERSONNEL

(List down the list of key personnel, which was submitted by the CONTRACTOR during tendering and approved by EMPLOYER).

ORGANISATION CHART

{Insert here the organization chart and CVs of the CONTRACTOR's site staff allocated to the project with the lines of communication and responsibilities. The CONTRACTOR submitted this information during tendering}.

ANNEX 'K'

SUB-CONTRACTORS AND ASSOCIATES LIST

(List below the names and addresses of the proposed sub-contractors and associates involved in the project, whom have adequate experience in carrying out similar works.)

ANNEX 'L'

CONTRACTOR's PROPOSED TEMPORARY FACILITIES ON SITE

{Insert here full description of the temporary facilities proposed by the Contractor for execution of the Works, such facilities shall include temporary accommodation for storing, tools, equipment, documents and site office furniture, all EMPLOYER needs to agree upon}

End of A4-Annexes

SECTION (B)

Technical Specifications

{List *down all the technical specifications, data sheets, Inspection sheets*}

End of section B- Technical Specifications

SECTION (C)

Bills Of Quantities/ Pricing Schedules

*(The Followings items 1 to 30,are applicable for
lump sum priced contract (if any))*

1. **Preambles**

1.1 All rates and lump sums shall be in *enter the Contract Currency.*

2. All rates and lump sums shall be fully fixed for the duration of the
   Contract and no fluctuations shall be permitted for any changes in any
   of CONTRACTOR's costs or inclusions, currency variation or any
   other reason unless expressly provided for elsewhere in this Contract.

3. Abbreviations

The following abbreviations, which appear on the attached Bill of
Quantities, shall have the following meanings:

-	B.O.Q.	Bill of Quantities
-	L.S.	Lump Sum
-	M2	Square Metre
-	M3	Cubic Metre
-	M	Linear Metre
-	No.	Number

4. EMPLOYER's working hours at SITE are set out in Section A2: 'Special Conditions'. CONTRACTOR shall be allowed to work outside the site working hours and days at the discretion of EMPLOYER subject to security and other rules at each location. All extra costs incurred through working overtime shall be included in CONTRACTOR's price.

5. Descriptions offered by EMPLOYER shall be for guidance only. CONTRACTOR shall be fully responsible for determining items and quantities as necessary for reaching the rated or lump-sum prices required for performing all CONTRACTOR's obligations under the CONTRACT.

6. CONTRACTOR shall be deemed to have included in his rates or sums for all waste, bulking or compaction factors, de-watering, over pulling and all other like elements or operations required to complete the WORKS, including all necessary measures to protect or preserve adjacent work or property during such operations, in accordance with the provisions of the Contract.

7. No re-measurement of Lump Sums or revaluation of any sort shall be permitted.

8. The Scope of Work, Specifications, Bills of Quantities and Drawings do not necessarily cover all items to achieve the requirements of the Contract. The Contract rates, however, shall be deemed to include all costs to execute the specified works and all related works, which an experienced CONTRACTOR shall reasonably foresee. Costs of items described or implied in the specifications and not specifically mentioned in the B.O.Q. shall be deemed included in the prices of the other items.

9. CONTRACTOR shall be required to complete, in full, his pricing inclusions in the columns provided.

10. Items not priced by CONTRACTOR shall be deemed included elsewhere.

11. CONTRACTOR shall fill in his prices as listed in the Bills of Quantities.

12. Should any new areas of work transpire which EMPLOYER considers are not envisaged as being part of this CONTRACT, quantities shall be measured by EMPLOYER. CONTRACTOR shall be given the opportunity, in such cases, to be present during the measurement. Prices for the new work, if any, shall be mutually agreed between EMPLOYER and CONTRACTOR.

13. No request shall be considered for an increase in the unit rates because they shall be inadequate to carry out additional work of a similar nature.

14. Except where otherwise detailed in the BOQ or specified, the rates and prices shall include all material supply and installation, tools and equipment, labour, supervision, transport, storage, installation works of the electricity and water from source to the site work, demolition/ construction/ erection/installation works, insurances, vacations, leaves, mobilisation, demobilisation, facilities, overheads, profits, taxes and duties, as mentioned otherwise, and whatever else shall be necessary for the execution and maintenance of the WORKS.

15. CONTRACTOR shall be deemed to have included for all the necessary information, details, clarifications or drawings and documents of the Contract.

16. The unit rates inserted by CONTRACTOR for the various items in the Bills of Quantities shall be used for the evaluation of interim payments and authorised variation orders, in accordance with the requirements of the Contract.

17. Accumulated debris or unusable materials shall be removed by CONTRACTOR to a suitable location off site designated by municipality or waste management authority. The cost of cleaning up and removal shall be deemed included in CONTRACTOR's rates.

18. CONTRACTOR shall be required to take all measures necessary to ensure that the whole of the WORKS shall be executed in such a manner as to minimise the generation of dust and other hazards.

19. CONTRACTOR shall, when directed by EMPLOYER, submit detailed supplementary schedules breaking down the rates for composite units of works in the Bills of Quantities into their component elements in such detail as shall be required by EMPLOYER.

20. Notwithstanding any limits which the wording of the individual items and/or explanations in the Preamble, shall imply, it shall be clearly understood by CONTRACTOR that the rates and sums, which shall be entered in the Bills of Quantities, shall be for the work finished complete in every respect. He shall be deemed to have taken full account of all requirements and obligations, whether expressed or implied, covered by all parts of the CONTRACT and to have priced the items therein accordingly.

21. All prices and rates shall include for preparation of proposals, drawings, calculations, documentation, etc. as shall be required for approval procedures.

22. CONTRACTOR shall provide at his own cost, means of access to work using scaffolding, trestles, ladders, brackets or whatever equipment the circumstances dictate with "safe" working as the major consideration. Where such access shall be erected or provided for CONTRACTOR's activities, CONTRACTOR shall permit reasonable utilisation and use of such facilities by others executing concurrent activities provided always that such permission and use should not cause delay or unreasonable hindrance or interruption of CONTRACTOR's own operations.

23. CONTRACTOR shall execute the WORKS in accordance with the specifications, drawings, manufacturer's instructions and to the instructions of EMPLOYER.

24. All lifting tackle, wire ropes, blocks, shackles etc. including any special equipment for executing the WORKS shall comply with the requirements of the appropriate British Standard Specification or ASTM or equivalent and carry a valid test certificate. Under no circumstances shall chain slings be used.

25. Where there shall be a possibility of damage to material equipment, or its deformation due to slinging from more than one point, ample strutting shall be provided to ensure that vertical lift shall be obtained.

26. No cutting away or welding of any parts of the WORKS shall be permitted unless with the written consent of EMPLOYER.

27. CONTRACTOR shall include for all temporary storage required by CONTRACTOR to store his materials etc., in accordance with the CONTRACT, and manufacturer's storage instructions. CONTRACTOR shall include for the protection and storage of sensitive material including pressurised and/or air-conditioned storage. The protection of all works and material shall be by CONTRACTOR whether these items are to be installed on the site or to be delivered to EMPLOYER's stores.

28. Unit Rates and Prices include for all safety measures requested by EMPLOYER including provision of metal screens and safety barriers and all measures necessary to protect adjacent items from the effects of overspray, paint spatter or drainage by impact. All such measures should satisfy EMPLOYER.

29. CONTRACTOR shall be deemed to have allowed for all effects on the execution and progress of works occasioned by climate and prevalent conditions and with specific reference to periods of high humidity and the incidence of snow/ wind/air borne dust occurring due to local climatic conditions..

30. CONTRACTOR's scaffolding and means of access shall be installed for a period prior to commencement of the work if required by EMPLOYER and shall remain until EMPLOYER inspection process

shall be satisfactorily completed. The period in either case shall not exceed one week.

31. EMPLOYER shall have the right to remove any item from the Scope of Work due to operational or safety requirements and the appropriate value shall be deducted from the Contract Price without any claim from CONTRACTOR.

2. **Bills of Quantities/Pricing Schedules** (*all rates in Contract Currency*)

S.NO.	DESCRIPTION	UNIT	QTY.	RATE	TOTAL
1					
2					
3					

TOTAL CONTRACT PRICE		*Contract Currency*	

End of section C- Bill of Quantities /Pricing Schedules

SECTION (D)

Drawings and Attachments

{List down all the drawings and attachments related to the Contract}

End of section D- Drawings and Attachments
End of the Sample of Construction Contract.

REFERENCES

(1) https://en.wikipedia.org/wiki/Roman_law

(2) Tolley's Commercial Contracts Checklists, by Rex Nwakodo, 2006.

(3) Strategic procurement –MENA conference 2010, by strategic procurement solutions LLC.

(4) Drafting contracts, by Tina L, Stark, ASPEN Publishers.

(5) MANUAL of purchases & tenders issued by Department of Finance / Abu Dhabi –UAE, EDITION Nov.2014.

(6) Purchasing and contracting guideline –procedures manual of Abu Dhabi Water & Electricity Authority (ADWEA), 2004.

(7) Law for Professional Engineer,3rd. Edition, by; D.L.Marston,

(8) Negotiation Journal July 1990, pp239-248.

(9) http://www.search.life123.com/web?q=Benefits+of+Alternative+Dispute+Resolution&qsrc=6&o=16149&l=dir

(10) http://www.iccwbo.org/court/english/arbitration.

(11) British Std. No; 4778, Part 3, section 3.1; 1991.

(12) Which FIDIC form to use seminar, by Cornerstone, www.corenstone-seminars.com

(13) FIDIC Construction Contract 2nd Ed (2017 Red Book)

(14) FIDIC Plant and Design-Build Contract 2nd Ed (2017 Yellow Book)

(15) FIDICEPC/ Turnkey Contract 2nd Ed (2017 Silver Book)

(16) Canadian Construction Documents Committee –CCDC 2 form-2008.

(17) Contract Drafting for Non-Lawyers Course, by Herb Wolfson, October 2010.

(18) Understanding Commercial Law in the UAE, by Herb Wolfson, December 2011.

Printed in the United States
by Baker & Taylor Publisher Services